# Domestic Threats

# DOMESTIC THREATS

JOSEPH HAYES III

Writers Advantage
San Jose  New York  Lincoln  Shanghai

# Domestic Threats

Writers Advantage
an imprint of iUniverse, Inc.

For information address:
iUniverse, Inc.
5220 S. 16th St., Suite 200
Lincoln, NE 68512
www.iuniverse.com

ISBN: 0-595-23912-9

Printed in the United States of America

*For my mother,*
*Joan Hayes.*

# Contents

# Acknowledgments

In grateful acknowledgment to my wonderful wife Beth, without her assistance with research as well as her unending encouragement and support, this book would not have been possible. I would also like to acknowledge, Mike Kochersperger, whose artful work graces the cover of *Domestic Threats*.

# Preface

Every American man, woman, and child has been taught that the Bill of Rights guarantees our freedom. But, such semantics repeated enough over two-hundred years have left us blissfully ignorant to reality. The Bill of Rights is a blueprint for freedom and two centuries after our founding it has become a symbol of that freedom. But there is no magic contained within that parchment. The magic is embodied in the American people, because we will only continue to enjoy our freedom as long as we are willing to fight for it.

While we can point to a specific date in 1776 when we declared our independence, we will never be able to point to any one date when we definitively won our freedom. Our quest for freedom is an eternal struggle that only began in July 1776 and has been waged everyday since. So far we have succeeded in winning most of those battles, but there have also been some losses and many casualties along the way. The players have changed many times over and the circumstances constantly differ, but the location of virtually all of our greatest battles for freedom have and will continue to be fought within our own borders.

Our hold on civil liberties is more fragile than most people realize and is only ever as assured as the integrity of the leaders we elect as its caretakers. This only serves to underscore the fact that living in a democracy is not just a spectator sport. Because in the final analysis, in a democracy where the people have the right to vote, you get what you vote for and thereby get what you deserve, nothing more and nothing less. This book presents 16 case histories contained within 14 chapters of some of the most fundamental civil liberties having been denied citizens of the United States.

At some point or another in our history our government has violated virtually every right ever promised to the people by the Bill of Rights. All three branches of our government have perpetrated laws, executive orders, court rulings, and just plain brute force—physical actions that were clearly unconstitutional. And there is no indication that these assaults on our freedom are decreasing even at this late date and time in our history.

In 1988, while campaigning for the presidency, George Herbert Walker Bush proudly boasted that if he were president, he would force all school children to recite the pledge of allegiance, despite what the United States Constitution or Supreme Court had to say about freedom of speech. Not only did this threat fail to raise much concern among the general public, he was cheered and rode a wave of popularity into the White House.

Twelve years of conservative rule in the White House by the Reagan-Bush administrations have left us saddled with one of the most conservative courts in history a full decade later, a court that has already demonstrated a propensity to take back with a sweep of their hand civil liberties, which took centuries to win.

The Renquist Court has already seen fit to no longer require police to advise suspects of their rights after arrest. This does not pose much of a problem for career criminals who probably know their rights better than the police, but could be disastrous for the occasional innocent person that might be arrested in error. They also ruled that search warrants guaranteed by the Fourth Amendment are now optional, giving the green light to police to violate the very breaking and entering laws they are supposed to be protecting society against.

The high court also announced their intention to dramatically cut back on their reviewing of "forma pauperis" cases, which are cases being appealed by people who cannot afford to pay the courts filing fee. This move in essence makes the kind of justice a person receives dependent upon how much they can afford. How this action could possibly serve to improve the country's judicial system or its fairness has been lost on almost everyone else in the legal community. In fact, many of the greatest landmark cases, which have helped to improve our judicial system, have come about via this route. And it is not difficult to imagine that acts of injustice would more likely be perpetrated against those who cannot afford to retain legal counsel of their own, as opposed to those who can.

The Renquist Court also increased the time a citizen can be held without being charged with a crime from 24 to 72 hours. This is longer than a person could have legally been held in the former "evil empire" of the Soviet Union. But even all of this was not enough for the Renquist Court. They also broke a two-hundred-year-old precedence by invading the bedrooms of America, holding in a 1986 ruling (see chapter XI) that states have the authority to make oral sex illegal and punishable by up to 20 years in prison even when engaged in by consenting adults in the privacy of their own bedrooms with the curtains closed and the door shut. By their actions, the Renquist Court has proven to be by far one of the most dangerous courts in our history.

But while conservative extremists have traditionally always perpetrated the most challenges to civil liberties, they by no means hold a monopoly on it. Contrary to popular belief, liberals are also capable of threatening our freedom. A good example of this is the popular liberal interpretation of the First Amendment's separation of church and state. Their interpretation is that prayers or any form of religious expression exercised by anyone in any public place should be banned. But this concept far surpasses any reasonable interpretation of separation of church and state. And in fact, becomes outright repression of freedom of religion, which is also prohibited by the same First Amendment.

In the final analysis the greatest threats to our freedom will never come from some evil, foreign, mustachioed dictator. Rather they will come from some very well meaning, patriotic Americans determined to save us from ourselves.

The greatest threats to our freedom are *Domestic Threats*.

# I

## Alien and Sedition—Act I

*"Eternal vigilance is the price of freedom."*

*—Thomas Jefferson*

The ink was barely dry on the Bill of Rights before the first major assault on it came. In the summer of 1798, as a result of growing hysteria over the possibility of war with France, the Federalists lead by President John Adams pushed through Congress a series of laws designed to curb dissent against the government. It was their opinion that by outlawing criticism of the government, it would somehow protect the country from an invasion from France. It was no coincidence that the government they were trying to protect was currently under their control, and was being challenged by the new Democratic-Republican Party. To the Federalists, both of these challenges—one domestic and political and the other foreign and somewhat exaggerated—were one and the same.

Until 1792, the Federalists were literally the only party in town, even as late as 1798 they continued to hold the balance of power in the United States. But, then they saw their hold on that power slowly starting to slip away.

The Federalists were not a political party per se, but rather one of two fundamental political schools of thought that prevailed immediately after the Revolutionary War. Those identifying themselves as Federalists were in favor of a strong federal government while the Anti-Federalists thought the states should retain most of the power, keeping the federal government weak thus making the United States a loose confederation of states. By the late 1790's most of the Anti-Federalists and some of the more progressive Federalists were now coalescing into the new Democratic-Republican party.

The Federalists played a major role in declaring Independence from Great Britain, winning the Revolutionary War, and setting up the new government—quite an impressive list of accomplishments for any one political affiliation. But with independence being won and the federal government being formed, they were fast outliving their usefulness. They ultimately proved to be much better at forming democratic governments than campaigning for election to that government. In stark contrast to the political parties of today, the Federalists were good statesmen and lousy politicians.

The Federalists ran the government with arrogance and high-handedness and were averse to the concept of scurrying for votes among the peasants. But that was exactly what was required to win election to the very government that they themselves created. They did not believe that poor, uneducated people were intelligent enough to determine who the leaders of the country should be.

The Federalists fought 'tooth-and-nail' during the constitutional convention to keep the bulk of electoral power out of the hands of the common man. While they had to accept some compromise they did succeed in winning two-thirds of the battle by empowering the state legislatures to elect the U.S. Senators and forcing the creation of a very peculiar institution called the Electoral College to elect the president. Only the election of the U.S. House of Representatives was left to the people.

The Federalists refused to solicit the opinions or approval of the people, but rather talked down to them, dictated to them, and never missed an opportunity to show their contempt for them. They attempted to maintain their eroding public support through ominous warnings that to trust the stewardship of state to anyone else, especially those who would pander to popular opinion would wreck the republic for sure. Specifically, they warned the people against trusting the Democratic-Republicans.

The Democratic-Republicans, lead by Thomas Jefferson, were much more oriented towards the common man, (i.e. the farmer), believing that the average person was capable of making the right decision if fairly and fully informed of the facts.

At this time in our history the actual concept of and even the word Democratic was still too radical a term to utter publicly, even by the Democratic-Republicans who typically referred to themselves as simply Republicans.

In the realm of foreign affairs, the new nation was having trouble commanding the respect due a sovereign nation. War was raging throughout Europe, principally between Great Britain and France. The U.S. was desperately trying to remain neutral. But at times, it seemed as if Britain and France were in a contest to each outdo the other in humiliating the United States. Both of these country's navies routinely stopped and boarded American merchant vessels. They seized the cargo and sold it off at admiralty sales and forced the American sailors to serve in their navy. Britain, however, far exceeded France with regards to these abuses.

The mood in the United States was sharply divided. There was still a great deal of popular resentment towards Great Britain left over from colonial days and admiration for France's support of our revolution. This opinion was strongly reflected by the Democratic-Republicans. However, the politically besieged Federalists looked across the ocean with great anguish at the remnants of the bloody and cataclysmic

French Revolution. France's revolution had just succeeded in over-throwing their monarchy and creating a Constitutional Republic similar, at least on paper, to the American one. The American Revolution inspired the French Revolution, but it was very different in its ferocity and vindictiveness.

The French Revolution ended up being class warfare, the prime targets of which were the aristocrats—the land owning, educated, moneyed class. Their executions became sport with as many as 40,000 people being slaughtered in the "reign of terror." This greatly concerned the Federalists, who were for all intents and purposes the American version of aristocrats.

The Federalists accused the Democratic-Republicans of being traitors and agents of France by attempting to incite a popular uprising against them and setting the stage for a French invasion. A popular uprising was indeed coming, though only politically, and was actually nothing more than leadership of the government about to pass from one political party to another for the first time.

It was against this backdrop that the Federalists, in their desperate bid to hold on to power, pushed through Congress a series of restrictive acts collectively known as the Alien and Sedition Acts.

The first such act passed the House of Representatives by a vote of 44 to 41 on June 16, 1798 and was titled the Naturalization Act. This act extended the required residency from 5 years to 14 years in order to become a citizen of the United States. One week later they passed the Alien Friend Act, which permitted the president to deport any alien suspected of treasonous intent. The Alien Enemies Act further supplemented this legislative coup on June 20, 1798, when it granted the president the authority to arrest any citizen of a foreign country and deport the person. Then three weeks after that, on July 11, 1798, a fourth piece of legislation was passed into a law known as the infamous Alien & Sedition Act, proper, which permitted the president to arrest any citizen of the United States who makes malicious or false statements against the government.

It was this last piece of legislation that most blatantly violated the First Amendment's guarantee of freedom of speech, as well as the Fifth Amendment's protection against being deprived of life, liberty or property without due process. And, as with most such cases of domestic threats, they were all grossly out of proportion to the actual threat at hand.

Many of the Democratic-Republicans voiced suspicion of the Federalists concerns of a French invasion as being nothing more than a political bogeyman designed to justify their attempts to silence political opposition. Thomas Jefferson expressed little fear of a French invasion, but a great fear of freedom of speech being outlawed by the Federalists here at home.

On Christmas Eve, 1798, the Virginia State Legislature passed a resolution sponsored by James Madison, which declared the Alien and Sedition Acts as null and void. The resolution went on to accuse the federal government of reneging on the guarantee of freedom of speech made by the Bill of Rights, which the states had made a precondition for joining the union. Kentucky promptly passed a similar resolution authored by Thomas Jefferson. Virginia and Kentucky then urged other states to follow suit. But their request fell on deaf ears, and Virginia and Kentucky stood alone.

The Federalists did in fact use the Alien and Sedition Acts against their political opponents and indictments were brought quickly, mostly against newspapers that were critical of President Adams and the Federalist Party.

Among those imprisoned under this law was Benjamin Franklin Bache, the grandson of Benjamin Franklin, for an article he published in his Philadelphia newspaper criticizing the president. A United States Congressman, Matthew Lyon, was also arrested and found guilty of violating the Alien and Sedition Act. He was fined

$1,000 and thrown in prison for criticizing the president on the floor of Congress.

On one of the first appeals made under this law, a Federalists judge responded to the argument that the Alien and Sedition Acts violated the guarantee of freedom of speech, by stating, "Americans cannot afford the luxury of discussing both sides of this question," adding "that all truths are not useful or proper and therefore should not be printed."

The Alien and Sedition Acts eventually sealed the fate of John Adams' presidency and his Federalist Party. The Republicans captured several seats in Congress and Thomas Jefferson was elected president in the election of 1800. Immediately after being sworn into office, President Jefferson pardoned all those convicted under the Alien and Sedition Acts and ordered Congress to repay all fines levied against them.

For generations of school children the Alien and Sedition Acts have been a comfortably distant example of how some of our most trusted leaders have violated the very constitution they swore to protect and uphold. But the battle for civil liberties goes on to this day. Even though we have always had sufficient laws forbidding espionage, sabotage, and treason and providing severe penalties for the commission of such crimes, there have been other times since 1800 when the Congress has passed other sedition acts amazingly similar to the original ones. This has typically happened during times of heightened tensions with foreign powers. In the final analysis, none of these laws ever contributed anything to keeping our shores safe from foreign invasion; they only proved efficient at suppressing political dissent at home.

# II

---

# Alien and Sedition—Act II

*"I disapprove of what you say, but I will defend to the death your right to say it."*

—*Voltaire*

Woodrow Wilson won his first term as president with a pledge of "new freedom," promising to protect civil liberties from infringements by the federal government. But just as his more famous boast of, "he kept us out of war" would ultimately ring hollow, so too would his promise to be the great defender of civil liberties. Wilson's administration would ultimately be responsible for the greatest assault on civil liberties in more than a century.

The world was a volatile place in 1917. The First World War was raging on in Europe with the United States about to enter into the alliance with Britain and France. The Bolshevik Revolution had just over-thrown the Czar and installed a communist regime in Russia. On the domestic front, labor unions were presenting an unprecedented challenge to the authority of the capital interests and there was no shortage of activity among some of the more radical political groups here in the United States. This included socialists and communists, each advocating that the United States adapt their form of government and the anarchists—who did not believe in any government at all.

The labor movement in this country was far removed from the radical political movements. Labor's objective was simply to improve the standard of living of the workingman through improved working conditions, pay and benefits. The capital interests and their supporters, however, sought to portray labor unions, socialists, communists and anarchists all as one and the same in an effort to discredit the labor movement and mobilize public opinion against them.

One young but influential proponent of that philosophy was a special assistant to the attorney general of the United States named John Edgar Hoover. He warned the attorney general that the United States government was in imminent danger of being overthrown by the trade unions, which he claimed were taking their marching orders directly from Russia via Russian immigrants in this country.

The United States government had initiated an aggressive public relations campaign designed to gain popular support for entering the war on the side of Britain and France against Germany. But in the process the American people were terrorized by grave pronouncements of imminent invasion of American shores by Germany, the threat of which was very much exaggerated. The American people were left so frightened that many of them began to arm themselves and most were more than willing to sacrifice some of their civil liberties for the false sense of security that the government was quick to offer in return.

Immediately after war was declared on April 6, 1917, the government initiated a total news black out. The resultant information void was quickly filled by even more rumors and hype.

Most of Wilson's Cabinet were calling for a massive round up of aliens, but Attorney General Thomas T. Gregory and Secretary of War Newton Baker opposed this effort as unnecessary. They were promptly accused of not being fully committed to the war effort and were quickly overwhelmed and overruled.

Prior to entering politics, Woodrow Wilson was a professor of political science and history at Princeton University. But apparently the professor either did not pay much attention to his own lessons or choose to ignore one of the most dramatic lessons of the first 150 years of the republic, namely how the undue restrictions of civil liberties invoked by the government via the Alien and Sedition Acts of the 1790's was both unnecessary and unconstitutional. As a result, he would be condemned to repeat these grievous errors almost verbatim.

Wilson's justice department actually resurrected most of the original Alien and Sedition Acts with just a few minor modifications then had them introduced in Congress as their own. *The Alien Act* was renamed the Enemy Alien Act, probably in the hope that by adding the word "enemy" it would dissuade any real debate on the actual details or the bill.

The new Enemy Alien Act made any alien male, 14 years of age or older, who wrote, printed, published or spoke any criticism against the government, Congress, official U.S. policy or any person in the military or civil service, liable to be apprehended, restricted, secured and removed as an alien enemy.

An amendment to the Immigration Act of 1917 was also passed, allowing the deportation of any alien who was involved with any organization determined to be radical by the justice department, without the need to prove the individuals' intent of any treasonous activity. This of course amounted to guilt by association. The fact that many people, especially lonely immigrants, joined organizations for purely social reasons without much concern about political opinions being raised by some of its members was not considered.

With the Enemy Alien Act being successfully passed without much opposition, the next step was to extend those restrictions of criticism to American citizens. So, on May 16, 1918, Congress passed the Sedition Act of 1918, which stated that anyone who uttered, printed, wrote or published any disloyal, profane, scurrilous or abusive statement about the United States government, government policy at the time, or, ironically, the Constitution of the United States including its guarantee of freedom of speech, would be subject to fines of up $10,000 and 20 years in prison.

The leader of the Socialist Party in the United States at the time, Eugene Debs, was one of the first to be convicted under the Sedition Act and was sentenced to 10 years in prison for making a speech in Canton, Ohio, denouncing U.S. involvement in the war. United States Congressman Victor L. Berger was also indicted for making pacifist statements against the war and was refused his seat in the U.S. House of Representatives. Thousands of other citizens whose only crime was to exercise their freedom of speech by disagreeing with America's entry into the war were also fined and jailed. The justice department actively encouraged vigilantism by creating the Justice Department Auxiliary known more popularly as the American Protection League (APL). Their membership eventually swelled to more than 250,000. With no training and little oversight they were given badges and turned loose on society with the expressed purpose of spying on their neighbors in an attempt to ferret out people considered to be disloyal to the country's war effort. They proceeded to round up any man of draft age on suspicion of being a draft dodger. And as might be expected with such a large and loosely supervised organization, many abuses were committed even beyond those sanctioned by the government.

The oldest and most respected veterans association today—the American Legion was founded in 1919 by returning veterans of the First World War. Immediately upon its founding a leadership council, the legion announced its commitment to actively fight communism. To demonstrate this commitment in November of 1919, the legionaries showed up at a socialist rally in Centralia, Washington. Once there, they proceeded to break up the rally. In the process they randomly grabbed one of the socialists, Wesley Everest, a World War I veteran himself, castrated him, hanged him, and shot him to death.

At first there was little outcry against all of this injustice. In fact most of these actions enjoyed the support of most of the public and the press. The *Washington Post* announced their support for the government actions by saying, "there is no time to waste on hair-splitting over infringement of liberty."

With the dramatic increase in activity due to the new Alien and Sedition Acts, the justice department expanded. Future FBI Director, J. Edgar Hoover, was appointed director of the new General Intelligence Division. Within 100 days Hoover conducted 60,000 investigations on members of radical groups, as well as many groups not so radical, such as the American Civil Liberties Union, congressmen, senators, cabinet members, judges, and anyone else who publicly criticized government policy, the president or Hoover himself. This was a practice Hoover would continue with ever increasing abuse until his death in 1972. He would eventually acquire files on nearly one million Americans.

In the process of Hoover's investigations much of what would be uncovered would not be of a criminal nature or a threat to national security at all, but rather just personally compromising. And Hoover quickly discovered the value of using this information for blackmail or leaking damaging material to the press, or employers to discredit or harass a person.

A. Mitchell Palmer became the new attorney general in March 1919. Palmer was a Democratic congressman from Pennsylvania and considered to be quite liberal for his time. But he would prove to be very impressionable at the hands of a master manipulator such as Hoover, who armed with his secret files, was urging massive roundups of aliens and dissident citizens in an attempt to avert the imagined overthrow of the government.

The justice department immediately began prepping the public for the upcoming raids by releasing grave pronouncements of labor unions being infiltrated by Bolsheviks who were bent on initiating a revolution similar to the recent one in Russia. Attorney General Palmer himself estimated that 90 percent of American radical movements were made up of immigrants.

The successful conviction of Eugene Debs gave the green light for further execution of the Alien and Sedition Acts. The attorney general gave the go-ahead for a massive nationwide dragnet, which would involve the round up of Russian immigrants. The Immigration Act of 1917, which permitted deportations without getting bogged down in the red tape of due process, would now be put to prolific use.

On November 7, 1919, federal agents and local police in several cities throughout the country—in what came to be known as the "Palmer Raids"—rounded up thousands of Russian immigrants. In New York alone, 200 arrests were made on just 27 warrants issued. Many of those arrested were not affiliated with any of the organizations in question and others were not even Russian immigrants, but rather American citizens. Suspects were dragged from their beds in the middle of the night, without any formal charges being filed. In Boston, captives were paraded through the streets in chains.

The next day the justice department proclaimed the dragnet a success and received widespread applause for thwarting the great revolutionary plot. Most people were so thoroughly convinced of the imminent danger of overthrow by the communists that little opposition was raised about the suspension of due process. Even the American Bar Association released a statement saying, "The threat of anarchy must be crushed in the United States at all costs."

With the first dragnet being so well received by the public, a second dragnet was quickly scheduled for January. Three thousand blank warrants were issued to federal agents to be filled in as needed. But even these 3,000 blank warrants were not enough for the number of arrests made this time, as ten-thousand people were taken in to custody.

In the process of the second dragnet federal agents raided a purported revolutionary meeting. They ended up arresting 39 bakers, which they released after finally being convinced that what they had actually raided was a co-op bakery. Demolition experts were called to the site of another raid to help identify confiscated diagrams, which turned out to be schematics for a phonograph.

The morning after the second dragnet, the first voices of conscience began to speak. The U.S. attorney in Philadelphia, Francis Kane, resigned in protest. Also some of the more liberal newspapers such as *The Nation* and *The New Republic* began to question the constitutionality of these mass round-ups. They were joined by some of the most notable law professors in the country such as Felix Frankenfurter, who would later become a Supreme Court justice. Slowly the public started to realize that the real peril was not immigrants or labor unions, but rather the heavy-handed tactics of the government. One man who objected to the new Alien and Sedition Acts, John Deney wrote, "What shall it profit us to defeat the Prussians if we prussianize ourselves?"

In May of 1920, Assistant Secretary of Labor John Abercrombie resigned to pursue a seat in the U.S. Senate and Louis Post was appointed to that position. He wasted no time in undoing what he saw as the great injustice of the mass roundups. He released thousands of the aliens rounded up in the "Palmer Raids" and reduced the excessively high bail set for many others. Hoover responded by publicly criticizing the undoing of his work, and ordered Post investigated.

In June 1920, Boston Judge George W. Anderson ruled the mass round-ups unconstitutional and ordered all 400 defendants arrested in that jurisdiction freed. He then chastised Hoover for his brand of domestic intelligence saying, "Government spies are no more trustworthy or unlikely to make trouble in order to profit themselves than spies of private industry. The spy system destroys trust and confidence and propagates hate." Hoover responded by questioning the judges' patriotism and ordering him investigated.

In September 1920, Max Eastman, editor of a small newspaper that was banned under the Sedition Act of 1918, said, "they give you 90 days for coveting the Declaration of Independence, six months for quoting the Bible, and pretty soon somebody is going to get life for quoting Woodrow Wilson in the wrong context." Congress eventually repealed the new Alien and Sedition Acts after seeing the unconstitutional acts for what they were.

Just as in the 1790's, the new series of Alien and Sedition Acts were nothing more than needless infringement of civil liberties under the guise of protecting national security. And once again, they proved to be far more dangerous than any threat presented by foreign nationals or dissident citizens.

# *III*

---

# Woman—The Discriminated Majority

*"It's a mystery how Jefferson could have written the Declaration of Independence and owned slaves. It's a mystery how the founders could write our Constitution and not allow women to vote. But we have taken the inner meaning and power of our founding documents and the spirit of America and breathed new life into them in each new generation."*

—*Al Gore*

At a time when it's considered remarkable to get one half of the eligible voters to turn out on Election Day, it's hard to imagine a time when people risked arrest and imprisonment fighting for that right. But this was exactly the price that was paid by women rights advocates in the late 1800's and early 1900's.

In 1776, New Jersey was the only state to permit women to vote, and at the Constitutional Convention of 1787, it was agreed that voter eligibility throughout the country would be left up to the states to decide. Then in 1806, as a result of an unexpected election outcome many believed was influenced by women voters, New Jersey decided to join the rest of the country in restricting suffrage to men only. And so it would be for the next century that women, who accounted for over 50 percent of the population in the United States, would be denied the right to vote.

In 1848, two strong-willed women named Lucretia Mott and Elizabeth Cady Stanton were refused their seats as delegates to an anti-slave convention because they were women. As a result of that slight they organized the first women's rights convention. This convention was held at the Wesleyan Church in Seneca Falls, New York, and marked the birth of the women's rights movement in the United States. Some 300 people, including 40 men, attended the convention. They outlined the injustices towards women, who at that time were considered to be more the property of a marriage than a partner in it. Women at that time, in addition to being denied the right to vote, were also not permitted to come and go as they pleased without the consent of their husbands.

Many of the freedoms being denied slaves at this time were also being denied women. In fact, legally there were few distinctions between women and slaves. Women were kept totally dependent on men by a whole host of restrictive laws. Husbands, even if legally insane, a convicted criminal or physically abusive, could still control all their property, have their wives' wages paid to them, and even sell their children without the wife's consent.

Elizabeth Stanton drafted a declaration of sentiments, calling for equal rights for women. The most notable and radical articles called for the right to vote. All of the attendees signed the declaration. But most of the signers later recanted their signatures under intense pressure and coercion from authorities, friends, and family. Elizabeth Stanton and Lucretia Mott were two of the few who stood firm in their conviction.

After the convention, Stanton and Mott continued to speak and write on women's rights. Profoundly influenced by Stanton and Mott's women's rights movement, a young schoolteacher named Susan B.

Anthony decided to take up the cause, jumping into the fray with a fervor that would eventually go almost beyond human endurance.

For the next several decades Susan B. Anthony would be a one-woman movement and, for many of those years, the lone advocate for women's rights. The name Susan B. Anthony would eventually become synonymous with the women's suffrage movement.

Always on the road, Susan B. Anthony endured atrocious lodging conditions; frequently sleeping in lice-infested boarding houses, barns, and fertilizer houses. She would endure it all just so she could preach the cause and take the inevitable abuse of hostile crowds that would throw rotten eggs and tomatoes at her and on occasion assault her as she ran from the gauntlet of hostile mobs.

Susan B. Anthony would speak at courthouses, schools, churches, and town squares across the country. She would pass out leaflets, lobby political leaders, and go door-to-door collecting signatures on petitions calling for a women's suffrage amendment to the United States Constitution. At first her petitions were ignored outright. But she never gave up. As soon as one legislative term ended she would start speaking, collecting signatures, and lobbying all over again. She was the first woman speaker most people had ever seen.

In the days before television or radio, political speeches and circuses were about the only form of public entertainment. Never feeling her public speaking was good enough; she continually sought out other celebrities of the day to also speak on the issue. Some of these personalities included: newspaper owner and future presidential candidate Horace Greeley, Senator Charles Sumner, and poet and writer Ralph Waldo Emerson.

Some of the strongest and most compelling opposition to the women's rights movement came from the clergy, who proselytized that according to the Bible, women were the servants of their husbands and their only duties were to their husbands and their children. They ominously warned that if women were granted voting rights it would destroy the marriage and wreak havoc upon the institution of the family. In spite of this by the late 1850's some states began passing progressive legislation concerning women's property rights and even some limited forms of suffrage. Then the Civil War came, and with the country's attention diverted, many of these laws were repealed.

In 1865, with the Civil War over and the slaves emancipated, Congress passed the 14th Amendment, which was designed to extend all of the protections of the Bill of Rights to the former slaves. As the states began holding their conventions to consider the amendment, many politicians who had previously committed to include women in the amendment were now reneging, reasoning that it would be too much to soon.

While the Fourteenth Amendment was being drafted, women's rights advocates specifically asked Congress to include women in it in an attempt to eliminate any ambiguities concerning them. When Congress finished, the amendment read, "No state shall make or enforce any law which shall abridge the privileges or immunities of any citizen of the United States." But then all of what was presumably given to women in this first section was taken away in the next section when the single word "male" was inserted in the right-to-vote clause.

Horace Greeley, who had previously advocated women's rights, quickly abandoned that unpopular position when he decided to jump into the political arena. When Susan B. Anthony testified before New York's Constitutional Convention on the 14th Amendment, Mr. Greeley asked her, "if given the right to vote would you be willing to fight in the next war?" To which Miss Anthony replied, "Yes, just as you fought in the last war—at the point of a goose quill." The chamber erupted in laughter.

Unfortunately, the lampooning Greeley took at the hands of Susan B. Anthony was only the beginning of his public embarrassment on the issue of women's rights. The next day the newspapers reported that one of the names on the petitions submitted by Susan B. Anthony was that of Greeley's own wife. Being totally outwitted and out-maneuvered he vindictively recommended that the word "male" not be removed from the amendment, claiming that militant feminists aside, most women did not really want the right to vote. The politician being out-politicked, Greeley then called Susan B. Anthony, "the most maneuvering politician in the state."

In 1868, the Fourteenth Amendment was ratified and for the first time the United States Constitution specifically denied women the full rights of citizenship. As a result of their defeat, women's rights advocates founded the National Women's Suffrage Association. The very next year, they succeeded in getting a resolution for women's suffrage introduced into Congress, though no further action was taken on it.

In 1870, the Fifteenth Amendment, which specifically addressed the issue of voting, was ratified. It stated, "The right of the citizens to vote shall not be abridged by the United States or any state on account of race, color or previous condition of servitude." Even though this amendment did not specifically mention women one way or another, the women's rights movement held the view that women, being citizens of the United States, fell under the umbrella of its protection.

The game of political volleyball with women's rights continued during the presidential campaign of 1872. As soon as Horace Greeley announced himself as the Democratic candidate for president, he immediately began attacking the women's rights movement. The Republicans, on the other hand, made an abrupt about-face from their past position and started speaking favorably about it. The Republicans even published a pamphlet titled, "Appeal to the Women of America," which urged women to work for the election of Ulysses S. Grant. Then just as abruptly as they came to ally themselves with the women's rights movement, the Republicans abandoned them and joined Greeley in attacking the movement as soon as it became apparent that Grant had the election sewn up.

Back at her home in Rochester, New York, Susan B. Anthony was determined to put the question of women's inclusion in the Fifteenth Amendment to the test by registering to vote in the upcoming election. On November 1, 1872, she and her three sisters went to their local polling place and demanded to be registered. The Registrar initially refused, citing New York state law. But Anthony countered by citing her presumed right to vote under the Fifteenth Amendment. After some debate, she was finally permitted to register. Not being satisfied with just her own registration, she then turned around and started rounding up other women to also register. Eventually she would have some fifty women registered.

On Election Day, Susan B. Anthony claimed to have voted straight Republican. But, her euphoria was short lived. Two days after the election a Federal Marshal showed up at her home and arrested her for illegally voting in that election. On December 23, 1872, she was arraigned in federal district court and her bail was set at $500, which she promptly refused to pay. She was thrown in jail, where she immediately wrote a Writ of Habeas Corpus, citing her detention as unconstitutional. But one of her defense attorneys paid her bail and she was released. On the way out of the courthouse, another attorney advised her that her release from custody had invalidated her Writ of Habeas Corpus and with it any hope of an early review of her case by the U.S. Supreme Court. She rushed back into the court and pleaded to cancel the bail, but was refused and returned home frustrated.

On June 17, 1873, Susan B. Anthony was tried in Canandagua, New York. Immediately after the opening arguments, Judge Ward Hunt, ruled the right to vote was for men only and directed the all-male jury to find a verdict of guilty. In a perverse reversal of roles, the judge gave the verdict to the court clerk, who recited to the jury, "You find the defendant guilty of the offense hereof she stands indicted, so say you all."

Susan B. Anthony was immediately on her feet protesting and asking that the jury be polled, which the judge promptly refused to do. The judge then dismissed the jury and fined Susan $100. Susan immediately replied that she would not pay a single dollar of the unjust penalty. But the judge refused to jail her again, effectively cutting off any hope of a further judicial review. With the judicial avenue effectively cut off, Anthony now knew that the only chance for women's suffrage lay in the political process.

The publicity of the case, however, dramatized the injustice towards women and the movement began gathering momentum. In 1876, petitions from 26 different states containing at least 10,000 signatures each were submitted to Congress calling for a women's suffrage amendment to the United States Constitution. These petitions were received with a great deal of sarcasm and laughter. Many politicians pointed out the perks of women, such as not having to work and being burdened with the other duties that come with the legal status accorded to men. They insisted that men were the real victims, ignoring the greater injustice of the situation. There was also a great deal of political concern at the time that if women were given the right to vote they would be the determining factor in passing prohibition laws.

In 1890, the Wyoming territory, which had already granted women the vote, applied for statehood. Debate on admitting Wyoming raged in Congress and it was generally agreed upon that Wyoming should be admitted, but that they should first limit suffrage to men only. The Wyoming legislature promptly transmitted a message stating that they would rather choose to stay out of the union than deny their women the right to vote. Wyoming was eventually admitted by a vote of 139 to 127.

In 1906, after more than fifty years on the stump for women's rights, Susan B. Anthony was asked of the chances of women's suffrage. She responded by saying, "It will come, but I will not live to see it. We can no more deny forever the right of self-government to one half of our people than we could keep the Negro forever in bondage." It was with that final assessment that she died on March 13 that year in New York at 86 years of age, having done more for women's rights than any other person before, during or since.

Elizabeth Cady Stanton and Lucretia Mott initiated the women's rights movement and Susan B. Anthony spent the next fifty years taking women's suffrage to the threshold of constitutional law. The final steps to suffrage that eluded Susan B. Anthony in life would be helped along by her memory after her death. It was only fitting that the women's suffrage amendment that would be passed fourteen years later would bare her name. As a further testament to her statesmanship, it was just as fitting that she would be one of few non-presidential personages to have her likeness appear on American currency with the release of the Susan B. Anthony silver dollar some sixty years later.

In 1910, Washington State voted in favor of women's suffrage, in 1911 California followed, and slowly the states started to fall one by one like old trees as momentum picked up even more for a federal women's suffrage amendment.

Shortly before her death, Susan B. Anthony met with President Theodore Roosevelt while he was still president. She urged him to use his immense popularity to endorse women's suffrage, and predicted that, if he did it, he would succeed. But even the foolhardy Teddy Roosevelt would not use the presidency as a "bully pulpit" to advance women's suffrage. Instead he reasoned that he had endorsed the idea while in the state legislature in New York decades before, he still supported it and was sure everyone knew of it, and therefore there was no reason to state so again. But during the election of 1912 when he was running as a third-party candidate, behind in the polls and desperate for support, he did state so again, endorsing women's suffrage and immediately following that pronouncement with a request that the women help elect him. The other two presidential candidates William Howard Taft and Woodrow Wilson remained unsympathetic.

But in 1912, after decades of betrayal by politicians with regards to women's suffrage, the movement was not about to put all of their trust in one, long-shot candidate to carry their standard. They started to campaign for themselves, staging a march in New York where 10,000 women participated. Shortly thereafter, three far away states, Oregon, Arizona, and Kansas, voted for women's suffrage.

On March 3, 1913, the day before Woodrow Wilson's inauguration, 8,000 suffragettes paraded in Washington D.C. But the chief of police there refused to provide police protection for the women. As a result, the women were attacked by angry mobs of men unsympathetic to their cause at several points along the parade route. The secretary of war calling out troops from Fort Meyers for crowd control was the only thing that saved the suffragettes from serious harm.

The women's suffrage amendment, which was now known as the Susan B. Anthony Amendment, was again introduced into Congress. President Wilson aggressively assumed the leadership of the country and control of the Democratic Party. But when asked to endorse the Susan B. Anthony Amendment, he waffled, saying that he could only follow his party on the issue.

By 1915, in what had by now become an annual event of presenting petitions to Congress calling for a federal women's suffrage amendment, over a half a million signatures were submitted. Another annual event—the women's rights parade in New York had 40,000 participants that year. At this point it did not take a political genius to see that the movement was picking up steam fast.

In his re-election campaign of 1916, President Wilson advocated letting the states decide for themselves the question of women's suffrage, while his Republican opponent, Charles Evans Hughs, included a federal women's suffrage amendment plank in the Republican Party platform.

Immediately after Wilson was elected to his second term, the suffragettes decided to turn up the heat on him by posting what they called "sentinels of liberty" in front of the White House. They vowed to picket around the clock, seven days a week until they were given the right to vote. As American troops were dispatched to Europe for the First World War, the women held up banners that read, "Democracy Should Begin at Home."

By June of that year, President Wilson had grown irritated by the women protesters and soon thereafter they started being arrested on the fabricated charge of obstructing traffic. The women, however, were not faint of heart and still refused to give up. Eventually some 200 women would be arrested for attempting to exercise their right to protest, a right of theirs that was not even supposed to be in dispute. They were fined and given sentences of between 30 and 60 days in "the work house," which the women's prisons were called in those days.

Once out of the public eye, they were separated from each other and kept in solitary confinement. They were interrogated for long periods of time without legal counsel and continually intimidated and threatened in an attempt to break them. One of the more frequent threats was that if they did not agree to cease their absurd demand for women's suffrage, they would be permanently transferred to an insane asylum.

The only thing that saved many of them from that horrendous fate was President Wilson finally acknowledging the inevitable and ordering most of the suffragettes quietly released. In July 1918, President Wilson finally endorsed the women's suffrage amendment and the very next day it passed the House of Representatives by a vote of 272 to 136. The remaining suffragettes were released from jail after a federal appeals court ruled their arrests and detention as being unconstitutional.

Meanwhile the vote for suffrage stalled in the Senate. The suffragettes immediately responded by moving their pickets to the front of the Senate building. The vote was taken again and this time fell just two votes shy. However, everyone by then knew that its passage was imminent. The Senate voted on the amendment again in early 1919 and was then just 1 vote shy of passage. Finally on June 4, 1919, one more

Senator saw the light, and then the amendment passed and was submitted to the states for ratification.

One by one the states, many of which had by then already passed their own suffrage amendment voted for the amendment. On August 18, 1920, Tennessee became the thirty-sixth state to ratify the amendment, making it the law of the land.

The women's rights movement was founded because women were denied the right to vote, denied equal pay, and denied other political, economic and social opportunities. Much of the fervor for the movement ended when the women's suffrage amendment became law in 1920. But even today, three quarters of a century later, many inequalities remain, though admittedly to a lesser degree and in more muted tones. Women still earn considerably less than their male counterparts. Most executive and managerial positions are still predominantly male bastions, and in 1992 as we celebrated the year of women, just 10 percent of the U.S. House of Representatives and five percent of seats in the United States Senate were held by women.

Slowly more and more doors are being opened. The often proposed and always ignored Equal Rights Amendment could have expedited matters by eliminating all of the inequalities that have existed from the beginning of the republic. The plight of the Equal Rights Amendment is a Catch-22 scenario and the perfect example of political double-speak. In spite of the many injustices that still exist in real life, opponents say that women already have equal protection under the Fourteenth Amendment, but then when this same amendment is cited by women's rights advocates, it no longer enjoys the same universal interpretation. And so the cycle continues.

# IV

## Frank "I am the law" Hague

*"Fear of serious injury cannot alone justify suppression of free speech and assembly. Men feared witches and burned women. It is the function of speech to free men from the bondage of irrational fear."*

—*Justice Louis D. Brandeis*

We have seen how some of those who have held political power in this country have sought to maintain or extend that power by denying civil liberties through convenient interpretations of the United States Constitution or by ignoring certain constitutional rights all together. But in Jersey City, New Jersey, in the 1930's there was a mayor who had amassed such complete political power in that city, as well as throughout the state, that he did not even bother trying to make things appear legitimate. He simply ran his city and even surrounding communities by edict, backed up by the brute force of his police department.

Protests, demonstrations and all other expressions of dissent were simply not tolerated within 10 miles of Jersey City. If the dissenters persisted the police were sent in to not only break up the demonstrations, but to break the heads of the demonstrators as well. Jersey City Mayor

Frank Hague was probably the closest thing we've ever had to a dictator in this country.

Frank Hague was a tall, partially balding man with a husky build that belied his 60 years of age. He was always immaculately dressed in dark suits, a pearl tiepin, and topped off with a derby hat.

Hague was born in the slums of Jersey City on January 17, 1876. He attended Public School #21 there, when he decided to show up for school. He was expelled from school in the sixth grade for various disciplinary problems. He was a tough street fighter and was quick to admit that he was a delinquent who never got caught. As mayor, he was known for his long and rambling speeches delivered with bad grammar.

He had a violent temper and would not hesitate to punch out a city worker, fellow politician or anyone else who did not readily agree with him. In heated arguments he would always intimidate opponents with gestures that threatened physical violence.

Mayor Hague's control in and around Jersey City was complete. More complete and effective in fact than that of any other political boss or machine in the United States, including the Pendergast machine in Kansas City, the Tammany machine of New York or even Huey P. Long's machine in Louisiana.

Hague controlled the newspapers and either paid off or intimidated any political opposition, effectively making Jersey City a one-man, one-party town. And he used the Jersey City police as his private army.

Hague first became active in politics in Jersey City's second ward at 18 years of age. He became Streets and Water Commissioner in 1911, which gave him jurisdiction over many of the municipal workers. He quickly moved to use the patronage of his office to hire workers that would promise total loyalty to him and he fired anyone already on the payroll who would not.

In 1913, he became public safety director, which gave him control over the city's police and fire departments. Again he hired or kept people who swore loyalty to him and purged the rest to gain control over these agencies, just as he had with the Streets and Water Department. Any policeman or fireman who did not toe the line was fined, suspended or fired and replaced with a new man who had no doubt about whom he owed his loyalty to. The result of all of this was that Frank Hague had amassed more control over the daily operation of the city than anyone else, including the mayor.

Hague's police tapped phones, opened and tampered with the federal mail, and arrested people for holding meetings or voicing opinions not shared by Hague. And whenever these more subtle means failed, a visit from Hague's police drove the point home with their nightsticks.

The Jersey City Police Department eventually became so bloated that there was one lieutenant for every 6 patrolmen. The city had the largest police force of any city of similar size in the country. As a result, Jersey City also had the highest taxes of any city in the country.

By 1915, for all intents and purposes, Frank Hague was already running the city; being elected mayor was only a formality and forgone conclusion. He was able to deliver reliable election results through his network of city employee votes, as well as their families' votes.

The voting block from Jersey City was instrumental in several critical county and state elections. Grateful legislators, as well as the governor himself, repaid Hague by sneaking in a generous pay raise for the commissioner. In addition, authority was given that allowed the commissioner full executive, legislative, and judicial powers in Jersey City, all of which was contrary to the whole concept of checks and balances between the branches of government.

In 1917, the same year the communists came to power in Russia, Frank Hague officially became mayor of Jersey City. By this time his control of the ballot boxes in Jersey City was absolute. Every city employee knew that their jobs depended on delivering the required votes. Furthermore, Hague did not shy away from actively using his police force to aggressively police all of the polling places within the city. Intimidation and ballot box stuffing were commonplace. And while these practices were not just restricted to Jersey City at the time, there was probably no other place were it was so widespread or brazen.

In 1919, the vote delivered by Hague's machine was instrumental in helping Edward I. Edwards become governor. As a reward, the governor appointed Hague men to many state positions including the bench, which would frequently be useful in protecting Hague from several court challenges in the future.

Hague would be largely responsible for electing the governor in the next four gubernatorial elections. In many instances the number of votes delivered by all of the wards in Jersey City exceeded the total number of registered voters there.

Hague won further loyalty not only by threatening jobs if votes were not delivered by voting blocks, which city employees were held responsible for, but also by seeing to it that generous pay raises were approved if they were delivered. The expense of all of this was passed on to the taxpayer. In return for the generous pay raises, city employees were required to pay anywhere from 3 percent to 10 percent of their wages to the mayor's campaign fund. If they refused, they were fired. But for most city employees, they were still ahead financially even with this deduction.

In the rare instance where the appropriate votes were not delivered, the ballots were either corrected or thrown out and replaced with the "right" vote.

During one election, about 250 members of the Honest Ballot Association, which were made up of students from Princeton University, came to Jersey City to witness the election. Several of the students were beaten up within the first hour of balloting. Most were bodily ejected from polling places. Some of the students went to Mayor Hague to complain. The mayor told them they could go back, but that they were on their own. He later bragged, "I told my boys to lay off, but it was a pretty dull election and they couldn't resist the temptation to have a little fun."

The mayor did not take criticism graciously. In 1937, when two congressmen who were critical of the mayor made it known that they planned on speaking in Jersey City, an ad appeared in area newspapers asking 800 veterans to show up at the rally with 2 feet of rubber hose. The implication was clear. When the congressmen did show up, the police immediately took them into "protective custody." In another example of his total control over the city and beyond, a United States Senator who was unfriendly towards the mayor was denied permission to speak at nearby Princeton University.

Anyone attempting to exercise their right to free speech that did not meet with the approval of the mayor, which was anyone that did not come to praise the mayor, was systematically and brutally routed by the police. They were typically beaten up, then either thrown onto the train or the ferry or shipped out of town. Or they might be arrested and thrown in jail, where they could linger for any length of time on charges of vagrancy, loitering or some other trumped-up charge.

The one newspaper that dared to criticize the mayor, *The Jersey Journal,* immediately had their property re-assessed, which went from $375,000 to $550,000. The mayor also implemented a very effective boycott of the paper by ordering all city workers and their families, which by then included most of the city, to not buy the *Journal* but instead to buy 4 copies of the rival newspaper. Most of the reporters and editors of the *Journal* were on the city's payroll as well. The editor of the *Journal* in fact happened to be a local judge, who Hague quickly threatened to impeach. As predictable, the criticism of the mayor came to a screeching halt. When negative articles of the mayor appeared in the *New York Post*, the mayor had all of the newspapers removed from newsstands within the city.

In 1929, with the depression fast approaching, the massive funding required to maintain Hague's political machine was in jeopardy. The mayor felt the need to draw more business into Jersey City. He succeeded in doing this by promising to keep the unions out of any business that came to Jersey City. And he kept his word. In 1936, he had forced through the state legislature New Jersey's Disorderly Persons Act, which stated that "anyone on foot or in any automobile…who cannot give a good accounting of himself…shall be considered present in this state for an unlawful purpose." This ambiguous law permitted the immediate arrest of people by police without provocation.

Pickets could be arrested and held for up to 90 days. In addition to this, the mayor made no bones about the fact that he was freely using violence against strikers, though he advocated that the strikers were all racketeers.

In 1930, the mayor had another ordinance passed that prohibited any hall rental, lease or use of any facility without a special permit being issued by the chief of police. Immediately upon review of this ordinance, the United States Supreme Court declared it unconstitutional. But the mayor, by now feeling untouchable, continued to enforce the law anyway. The mayor forbade any public assembly on the streets, highways, parks or public buildings, without a permit for "safety reasons," for fear of riot, disturbances or disorderly assemblies. Nightstick-wielding police barred all newspaper reporters, photographers, writers and civil rights advocates from any locations where strikes or demonstrations were occurring.

On December 31, 1933, two members of the Workers International Relief Fund went to the local Ukrainian Hall to solicit funds for starving miners. They were followed into the hall and promptly arrested by police for disorderly conduct. When two other men came to police headquarters to arrange for their counsel, they were arrested for loitering and not being able to give "a good accounting of themselves." All four men were held for one week without bail being set.

On July 16, 1933, a man approached a police officer in Jersey City to ask directions. The officer asked the man where he lived. "New York," the man replied. Without further provocation, the officer searched and arrested him, saying "that he was in a pretty out of the way place for a man with good intentions." And added, "A good man doesn't wear a hat like this, does he?" The man was thrown in jail for one day, presumably for wearing an illegal hat.

The mayor held a unique view of civil liberties, which he elaborated on one day in a city council meeting. "Whenever I hear a discussion of constitutional rights, free speech and the free press, every time I hear those words, I say to myself, that man is a red, that man is a communist. You never heard a real American talk in that manner."

On one occasion in 1937, workers at one business walked out on strike at 11:50 a.m. and were served with an injunction against any demonstrations, picketing, union meetings or handing out of leaflets at 11:57 a.m. The issuance of this injunction meant that the judge reviewed all affidavits, drew up injunction papers and had the injunction issued, all in just seven minutes. An accomplishment not witnessed in the American judicial system before or since.

On November 29, 1937, the Congress of Industrial Organizations (CIO) was attempting to inform the workers of Jersey City of their rights by distributing handbills. The police stopped them and seized their literature. They arrested 12 of the leaders and rounded the rest up and put them on the ferry to New York, even though many of them were residents of Jersey City, all done under the provisions of the Disorderly Persons Act. The police then blockaded the CIO headquarters. After a little persuasion on the part of the mayor's office, the CIO was unable to find any halls or grounds in the entire city to hold their meetings. So they announced an open-air meeting on December 17, 1937. But a city ordinance required a special permit for such meetings and the city promptly refused to issue one.

Hague pulled the strings of all of the local newspapers, which promptly responded by overwhelmingly supporting the mayor's opposition to the CIO and praising him as "the protector of the people." In addition to this, after some polite reminders to many area churches that the pro-Hague financial institutions held their mortgages, even they began to support the mayor's actions, and sermons praising the mayor's stand began to come from many of the pulpits throughout the city.

The CIO petitioned the court for an injunction, which was granted. The city appealed the injunction to the Court of Appeals. The mayor himself testified for three days during June 1938 in U.S. District Court. Hague at this point had amassed so much political power in all branches of the government that he believed he had total immunity from the law. Because of this confidence and a seemingly courteous opposition attorney who asked him to explain how government really works, the mayor proceeded to spill his guts on the stand, frequently answering questions over the objections of his own counsel. He was both candid and cocky. When asked about some of the seemingly obvious violations to constitutional law, the mayor arrogantly boasted that, "in Jersey City, I am the law." A boast that hence forward earned him the moniker of Frank "I am the law" Hague.

Upon appeal, the United States Supreme Court upheld the injunction against both the Disorderly Persons Act and the Jersey City permit ordinance. Mayor Hague would continue to hold on to power for several years after the court's rebuke of his strong-arm governing tactics. But it did mark the beginning of the end of his police state and the first step in bringing Jersey City back into the United States of America.

# V

---

## With Liberty and Justice for All

*"Patriotism is the last refuge of the scoundrel."*

*—Sam Johnson*

Mr. and Mrs. Walter Gobitis and their two children were Jehovah's Witnesses who lived in Minersville, Pennsylvania in 1936. The children, 12 year-old Lillian and 10 year-old William, attended the public school there.

As part of the daily routine at the Minersville School, as in all public schools throughout Pennsylvania, the day began with the teacher leading the class in reciting the pledge of allegiance. But Lillian and William Gobitis felt that saluting the flag was against the strict religious doctrine taught by their church. Specifically, their literal interpretation of the book of Exodus, which commands, "Thou shalt not make unto thee any graven image…thou shalt not bow down thyself to thee nor serve them." The Gobitis children felt that the flag was such a graven image and expressed their concern to their parents, who agreed with them.

They returned to school the following day, but refused to participate in the salute to the flag with the rest of their class. They were immediately removed from class and sent to the principal's office where they explained the reason for their actions. Unimpressed with their religious belief, the principle suspended them and referred the case to the Minersville Board of Education.

Upon review, the board felt that the flag salute was a school rule, which they had a right to mandate. The superintendent of the board of education delivered the ultimatum in person to Mr. and Mrs. Gobitis, stating that failure to comply with the school's rule would result in the children's expulsion from school.

Without hesitation, Mr. Gobitis' response was, "So be it." The Gobitis' immediately won the full support of their church and filed suit against the Minersville Board of Education. The two main points of contention in the lawsuit were that as school attendance in Pennsylvania was mandatory, the board of education was in fact forcing them to violate the law by expelling the children. And although Mr. and Mrs. Gobitis held no contempt for the salute to the flag taking place, they did not feel that their children should be forced to participate in light of the fact that compulsion to do so was in violation of their freedom of religion.

When the case came up before the U.S. District Court, the judge upheld the school board's right to enforce such rules. This decision was further upheld on review by the Court of Appeals. The Gobitis' did not give up, but instead continued to appeal their case all the way to the United States Supreme Court.

It was April 1940 by the time the case reached the Supreme Court and war was raging throughout Europe and in the Pacific. And while the United States was still over a year away from entering the war itself, feelings of nationalism and patriotism were already running deep throughout the country. Anyone showing the slightest lack of patriotism was prone to ostracism and branded a traitor.

The attorney arguing the case on behalf of the Gobitis children stated simply that "forcing the (Gobitis children) to recite the 'pledge of allegiance' against their religious belief was quite clearly a violation of their First Amendment, right to freedom of religious expression. And that denial of such freedom was along the same lines as those freedoms currently being denied the people of Germany and their occupied territories in Europe, by Hitler, found so distasteful by us here in America."

Remarkably the court remained unmoved, apparently opting on the narrowest interpretation of the First Amendment. The Minersville Board of Education's right to mandate the flag salute over religious freedom was upheld by an eight to one vote. Justice Frankfurter delivered the opinion of the Court stating, "…the question remains whether school children, like the Gobitis children, must be excused from conduct required of all other children in the promotion of national cohesion. We are dealing with an interest inferior to none in the hierarchy of legal values. National unity is the basis of national security.

"We live by symbols. The flag is the symbol of our national unity, transcending all internal differences, however large, within the framework of the Constitution. That the flag-salute is an allowable portion of a school program for those who do not invoke conscientious scruples is surely not debatable. But for us to insist that, though the ceremony may be required, exceptional immunity must be given to dissidents, is to maintain that there is no basis for a legislative judgment that such an exemption might introduce elements of difficulty into school discipline and cast doubts in the minds of the other children which would themselves weaken the effect of the exercise."

Justice Stone was the lone dissenter, and wrote, "Two youths, now fifteen and sixteen years of age, are by the judgment of this court held liable to expulsion from the public school and of all publicly supported educational privileges because of their refusal to yield to the compulsory law, which commands their participation in a school ceremony contrary to their religious convictions. They and their father are citizens and have not exhibited any action or statement of opinion of disloyalty to the government of the United States. They are ready and willing to obey all its laws, which do not conflict with what they sincerely believe to be the higher commandments of god. It would be a denial of their faith as well as the teachings of most religions to say that children of their age do not have religious convictions.

"The guaranties of civil liberty are but guaranties of freedom of the human mind and spirit and of reasonable freedom and opportunity to express them. The very essence of the liberty, which they guaranty is the freedom of the individual from compulsion as to what he shall think and what he shall say, at least where the compulsion is to bear false witness to his religion. If these guaranties are to have any meaning they must, I think be deemed to withhold from the state any authority to compel belief or the expression of it where that expression violates religious conviction, whatever may be the legislative view of the desirability of such compulsion.

"The Constitution may well elicit expressions of loyalty to it and to the government which it created, but it does not command such expressions or otherwise give any indication that compulsory expressions of loyalty play any such part in our scheme of government as to override the constitutional protection of freedom of speech and religion. And while such expressions of loyalty, when voluntarily given, may promote national unity, it is quite another matter to say that their compulsory expression by children in violation of their own and their parents religious convictions can be regarded as playing so important a part in our national unity as to leave school boards free to exact it despite the constitutional guarantee of freedom of religion.

"The Constitution expresses more than the conviction of the people that democratic processes must be preserved at all costs. It is also an expression of faith and a command that freedom of mind and spirit must be preserved, which government must obey, if it is to adhere to that justice and moderation without which no free government can exist."

The Gobitis case was widely reported. The Court's decision was especially fateful for Jehovah Witnesses, in that it was perceived by many as a green light for atrocities, much like Gobitis' attorney had warned of.

The plight of many of the Jehovah's Witness, who sought to hold their ground on practicing their strict religious doctrine, was severe and most un-American.

Just one week after the high court's ruling, a mob of several hundred "patriotic Americans" sacked and burned a Jehovah's Witness church in the little known town of Kennebunkport, Maine. This was followed by several other similar attacks throughout the country.

Some local police forces did their best to protect the Jehovah's Witnesses, such as in Litchfield, Illinois, where the police locked up about 50 Jehovah's Witnesses in the jail, as the only means of protecting them from lynch mobs. In Richmond, West Virginia, however, the police were just as bad as the mobs. The chief of police there had seven Jehovah's Witnesses force-fed castor oil in an attempt to force them to recite the pledge of allegiance.

In 1942, the State of West Virginia passed a law mandating all teachers and students in the state salute the flag, and provided ridiculously harsh penalties for any violation. This law was based largely on the foundation of the Gobitis ruling. Under the provisions of this law many Jehovah's Witness students were expelled from school and threatened with incarceration in reformatories. Their parents were threatened with fines and prison terms for contributing to their children's acts of delinquency.

But Jehovah's Witnesses in West Virginia stood firm in the face of many such harsh and unfair laws and violent attacks. The courage exhibited by many of them, while fighting what outwardly appeared to be patriotism, but was in fact radical nationalism, was as heroic and patriotic as any action in our history and certainly more patriotic than the actions of their attackers.

Throughout the country angry mobs broke up many Jehovah's Witness meetings and services. Some Jehovah's Witnesses were so severely beaten that hospital treatments were required. Many of their churches were torched. Some states even went so far as to pass laws outlawing the entire religion of Jehovah's Witness, an even more blatant violation of the letter and intent of the First Amendment.

One Jehovah's Witness in West Virginia, Walter Barnette, bloodied, but unbowed, filed suit seeking an injunction against the West Virginia law as unconstitutional in violation of his freedom of speech and religion. The U.S. District Court there ruled in his favor stating, "The Fourteenth Amendment as applied to the states protects the citizen against the state itself and all of its creatures, including school boards." The Board of Education immediately appealed the ruling and by 1943 the whole thing ended up back on the doorstep of the United States Supreme Court again.

On June 14, 1943, which ironically was "Flag Day," the Supreme Court finally paid fitting tribute to the true meaning of the flag by overturning their previous Gobitis ruling and declaring the Virginia law unconstitutional in an attempt to undo the great wrong which they had done three years earlier. This was the fastest the United States Supreme Court had ever overturned one of their own previous decisions.

Justice Jackson delivered the opinion for the Court stating, "A person gets from a symbol the meaning he puts into it. This case is made difficult not because the principles of its decision are obscure, but because the flag is our own. Nevertheless, we apply the limitations of the Constitution with no fear that freedom to be intellectually or spiritually diverse or even contrary will disintegrate the social organization.

"To believe that patriotism will not flourish if patriotic ceremonies are voluntary and spontaneous instead of compulsory is to make an unflattering estimate of the appeal of our institutions of free minds....freedom to differ is not limited to things that do not matter much. That would be a mere shadow of freedom. The test of its substance is in the right to differ as to things that touch the very heart of the existing order."

With this ruling came the end of the worst case of religious persecution in twentieth century America. But, the fight for freedom never ends. Half a century after the Jehovah's Witnesses were persecuted over their religious belief a resident of the same aforementioned Kennebunkport, Maine, would be a candidate for president of the United States. Despite the atrocities of blind patriotism demonstrated in the hometown of his youth, George Bush would attempt to resurrect the same issue of compulsory flag saluting that the Supreme Court struck down as unconstitutional in 1943.

In the presidential election of 1988, George Bush stood before several American flags furling in the breeze and accused his opponent, Massachusetts Governor Michael Dukakis, of being "a card-carrying member of the ACLU." The implication being that the ACLU specifically and civil libertarians in general were somehow enemies of America. George Bush then proceeded to criticize him for abiding by a court order that struck down a state law requiring compulsory reciting of the pledge of allegiance by all public schools students. Mr. Bush then stated he would have ignored the court order and presumably the First Amendment.

George Bush either did not understand what the First Amendment to the United States Constitution meant or worse yet, did understand it but decided to resort to whatever politics would win, freedom of speech and religion be damned. Whatever his reason and in spite of his threat, he would be elected president of the United States in 1988.

# VI

---

# The American Concentration Camps

*"When Hitler attacked the Jews, I was not a Jew, therefore, I was not concerned. And when Hitler attacked the Catholics, I was not a Catholic, and therefore, I was not concerned. And when Hitler attacked the unions and industrialists, I was not a member of the union and I was not concerned. Then Hitler attacked me and the Protestant church and there was nobody left to be concerned."*

—*Pastor Martin Niemoller*

War is a frightening thing. The anxiety of war manifests itself by fear, anger, hate, and an intense and frequently irrational prejudice against those of our own citizens whose appearance, names or national origin resembles that of the enemy.

No group of American citizens was more victimized by the anxiety of war than Japanese-Americans during the Second World War. This anxiety manifested itself with the most massive revocation of civil liberties by the United States government in history of 120,000 of our own citizens.

The surprise attack on Pearl Harbor on December 7, 1941, shocked the nation. In the days following the attack, the FBI conducted investigations into the risk of espionage and sabotage by Japanese-Americans, particularly on the Pacific Coast. After an intensive three-month-long investigation, J. Edgar Hoover reported to the war department and President Roosevelt that no credible threat regarding Japanese espionage or sabotage on the Pacific Coast was found. Naval intelligence also submitted at the report, which stated that no attack on the West Coast of the United States was imminent. Despite these reports, several generals almost immediately began suggesting mass round-ups of Japanese-Americans.

Some in the administration were concerned about the mass tramping of civil liberties for no good reason. Secretary of War Henry Stimson stated, "we cannot discriminate among our citizens on the ground of racial origin alone." He further warned that, "any forced removal of Japanese-Americans would tear a tremendous hole in our constitutional fabric." Harold Ikes and Attorney General Francis Biddle told the president that the FBI and the military had offered no justification for mass evacuations. FBI Director J. Edgar Hoover even suggested that, "the Army was getting a bit hysterical." One suggestion made was to declare martial law on the entire West Coast and suspend writs of habeas corpus (a legal challenge against being held without good reason or due process).

Assistant Secretary of War John J. McCloy dismissed the Constitution as, "just a piece of paper." He elaborated on his strategy to bypass the Constitution, explaining that military commanders already had the legal authority to move or eliminate anyone from a military reservation they deem necessary without having to suspend habeas corpus or worrying about a rat's nest of other constitutional issues. So he suggested declaring the entire Pacific Coast a military zone and then delegate it to the Army to handle.

The passions of war in light of the casualties of Pearl Harbor quickly overwhelmed the government and fanned the flames of prejudice. The commander in charge of the West Coast, General Dewitt, stated in a congressional hearing that a "Jap is a Jap." California

Congressman Leland Ford demanded in that "all Japanese, whether citizens or not, be placed in inland concentration camps." And newspaper columnist Westbrook Pegler demanded that the government immediately place all Japanese-Americans under armed guard and "to hell with habeas corpus."

Taking the Assistant Secretary of War McCloy's suggestion, President Roosevelt signed Executive Order 9066 on February 19, 1942, designating the entire West Coast of the United States a military area.

At first a curfew exclusively for Japanese-Americans was imposed. Shortly thereafter, the wholesale detention and relocation of an entire race of people, most of whom were American citizens, both naturalized as well as native born. When Japanese-Americans were relocated they were forced to leave most of their possessions and property, including, in many cases, whole businesses behind, without compensation. They had identification tags attached to their clothing and were crowded into cattle cars for transport to the camps.

Anyone of Japanese ancestry was ordered to report and register at an evacuation center by hand bills and radio advertisement. Most voluntarily complied. Unbeknownst to most people, the United States government at this point broke a long-standing covenant with the people and used census data to identify Japanese-American citizens.

Major Bendetsen, the military's author of Executive Order 9066 that effectively transferred jurisdiction of the Japanese-American issue from the justice department to the war department, was given two promotions in two weeks and put in charge of the relocation effort.

A Catholic orphanage contacted Colonel Bendetsen stating that they had some children of Japanese descent, as well as others that were half-Japanese. The colonel was asked which of those children should be sent to the relocation center. The colonel was reported to have said that, "I am determined that if they have one drop of blood of Japanese in them, they must go to the camp."

The government gave them innocuous names like assembly centers and relocation centers, but they were in fact American concentration camps plain and simple. They were austere military camps quickly and inadequately constructed in the deserts and wastelands of Middle America. Each camp had about 450 wood and tarpaper buildings divided into blocks of 20 much like a prison cellblock. For each block of buildings there were just two laundry and bathing facilities. The camps were surrounded by barbed wire and guarded by armed solider. The guard towers were equipped with searchlights and machine guns.

Several camp shootings of prisoners by guards are known to have taken place under questionable circumstances and resulting in only the most cursory of investigations. In one—instance, two seriously ill prisoners, Hirota Isomura and Toshio Kobata, were being transferred from the internment camp at Fort Lincoln in Bismarck, North Dakota, to the Lordsburg internment camp in New Mexico along with 150 other prisoners. The prisoners were forced at bayonet point to march from the train station to the camp. Because of their illness, Isomura and Kobata were transported by truck.

The details were never made public, but shortly after their arrival at the front gate, other inhabitants of the camp heard gunfire. Isomura and Kobata were never heard from again. When their friends arrived and asked about them, they were told the doctor was treating them. When they inquired about them again the next day, they were told that they were both shot during an escape attempt while on their way to the camp. Their friends found this difficult to believe due to the illness and weakness, which made walking to the camp—much less running— from the camp impossible. But no further explanation or details were ever provided.

The next day when two other prisoners were digging Isomura and Kobata's graves, they were told by one of the guards, "these graves are for the Japanese who died; if you don't do your work quickly, I will make you dig two more."

Three cases pertaining to the internment of Japanese-Americans would make their way to the United States Supreme Court over the next few years. The first, Hirabayashi vs. United States, began on May 16, 1942. Gordon Hirabayashi, a University of Washington senior, went to the FBI headquarters in Seattle, Washington, and stated that by being a native-born American citizen he was refusing to register to be relocated due to his belief that that would violate the due process clause of the Fifth Amendment. An FBI agent there tried unsuccessfully to talk Hirabayashi into voluntarily going to the relocation center, but when he continued to refuse, he was arrested.

Gordon Hirabayashi spent five months in the King County Jail before his trail in October 1942, where Judge Lloyd Black dismissed the argument of his detainment being a violation of his Fifth Amendment rights as being a "technical interpretation." The judge then proceeded to brand all Japanese as being "unbelievably treacherous and…ruthless."

Judge Black then instructed the jurors to find the defendant guilty. Ten minutes later the jury did what they were told, and parroting the judge's words, returned a guilty verdict. Bail was denied and Hirabayashi was returned to jail.

Fred Korematsu was a 20-year-old American citizen of Japanese ancestry born in Oakland, California, and was a welder at a San Francisco ship-yard when Pearl Harbor was attacked. He did not want to be relocated. He evaded registering for relocation by continuing to work under an alias name impersonating a Mexican. Korematsu was eventually found out, tried, and summarily found guilty. He was sentenced to five years probation to be served in an internment camp.

A man during this time by the name of Minoru Yasui was an Oregon lawyer and officer in the United States Army Reserve. Understanding the constitutional ramifications better than most, he intentionally violated the registration and relocation order. Yasui went out of his way to get arrested in hopes of quickly challenging a law he knew to be unconstitutional. He succeeded on getting arrested in Portland, Oregon, on

March 28, 1942. But, Yasui could never have imagined what lay in store for him as a result. He was summarily found guilty by Judge James Alger Fee, sentenced to one-year imprisonment, fined $5,000 and denied bail.

Yasui would serve the next nine months of his sentence in solitary confinement in a jail in Portland, Oregon. He was not permitted to bath, shave or get a haircut for months after his incarceration. His nails grew so long they curved around his fingers and toes. He stated he tried to trim them by chewing them as best he could. Solitary confinement is typically reserved as a form of punishment for only the most dangerous or unruly prisoners. But, Yasui was in solitary confinement for no other reason than insisting on his civil rights, which were supposed to be guaranteed to him by the United States Constitution.

The Supreme Court reviewed the Yasui and Hirabayashi cases in June of 1943 and ruled to uphold their convictions and continue the interment of Japanese-Americans as the Army saw fit. Chief Justice Harlan Fiske Stone wrote the decision for the court stating on the one hand that racial discrimination was "odious to a free people" and as such is a denial of equal protection. But went on to say, "The successful prosecution of the war may justify actions which places citizens of one ancestry in a different category from others."

Eighteen months later, Korematsu's conviction was upheld by a 6-3 ruling by the United States Supreme Court. Justice Black delivered the court's opinion. "We uphold the exclusion order as of the time it was made and when the petitioner violated it...In doing so, we are not mindful of the hardships imposed by it upon a large group of American citizens...But hardships are part of war and war is an aggregation of hardship."

Justice Frank Murphy wrote the dissenting opinion stating that; "All residents of this nation are kin in some way by blood or culture to a foreign land. Yet they are primarily and necessarily a part of the new and distinct civilization of the United States. They must accordingly be treated at all times as the heirs of the American experiment and as entitled to all of the rights and freedoms guaranteed by the Constitution....to infer that examples of individual disloyalty prove group disloyalty and justify discriminatory action against the entire group is to deny that under our system of law, individual guilt is the sole basis for deprivation of right."

He went on to state that the forced expulsion of American citizens from their homes "goes over the brink of constitutional power and falls into the ugly abyss of racism..."I dissent therefore from this legalization of racism."

It would not be until forty years later that the United States government would finally acknowledge the wrongfulness of the forced relocation and detention of Japanese-Americans during the Second World War. On August 10, 1988, President Ronald Reagan signed the Civil Liberties Act of 1988. This act was passed by Congress to provide a presidential apology and payment of $20,000 to the internees, evacuees, and persons of Japanese ancestry who were denied liberty or property due to the discriminatory action by the United States government during World War Two.

# VII

---

## Illegal Search and Seizures

*"Individual rights are not subject to a public vote."*

—*Ayn Rand*

Early one spring morning in 1957, a bomb exploded in front of the home of Cleveland, Ohio, boxing promoter and gambler Don King. Several days later, Cleveland police received an anonymous tip that the perpetrator of that bombing was hiding at a home on Milverton Road.

Cleveland police immediately converged on the reputed hide out, which was owned by Dollree Mapp. Three policemen knocked on Ms. Mapp's door and asked to search her home. Unsure of what to do, Ms. Mapp called her lawyer and on his advice refused to let them in without a search warrant. The police returned to their cars and staked out her house. Three hours later seven policemen appeared on Ms. Mapp's doorstep and stated they had a search warrant. Ms. Mapp asked to see it, at which time one of the officers flashed what Ms. Mapp contended was a blank piece of paper. She grabbed the paper and stuffed it down her blouse. The policemen grabbed and restrained her, retrieved the paper and then handcuffed her.

Mrs. Mapp was then held in her bedroom while the police searched the house. In the process of the search, the police found and arrested a man in the house who they believed was the suspected bomber.

After arresting the man, the police continued to search the house. In the course of that search, the police gathered up a few books from a box in the basement, some pictures from her dresser drawer and paper with some doodling on it, all of which they deemed to be obscene material. They then arrested Ms. Mapp and charged her with possession of pornographic materials.

Dollree Mapp was subsequently tried in Ohio State Criminal Court and found guilty of violating Ohio's anti-pornography law which stated, "No person shall knowingly...have in his possession or under his control any obscene, lewd, or lascivious book, magazine, pamphlet, paper, writing, advertisement, circular, print, picture...or drawing...of an indecent or immoral nature. Whoever violates this section shall be fined not less than two hundred nor more than two thousand dollars or be imprisoned for not less than one nor more than seven years, or both."

Under such a broad definition as Ohio's anti-pornography law, most medical books and many of the world's most renowned works of art would be illegal.

At her trial, the police were unable to produce the search warrant, which resulted in Dollree Mapp's arrest, claiming that it had somehow been misplaced. But even if police had obtained a totally legitimate search warrant, it would have only authorized a search for the bombing suspect and not a fishing expedition for "obscene materials."

Ms. Mapp claimed that the obscene material, which the police confiscated, belonged to a man from New York who had rented a room from her some time ago and were left there by him. This claim was corroborated by the testimony of a friend of Ms. Mapp's.

The Fourth Amendment states, "The right of the people to be secure in their persons, houses, papers, and effects against unreasonable searches and seizures shall not be violated and no warrants shall be issued, but upon probable cause, supported by oath or affirmation, and particularly describing the place to be searched, and the persons or things to be seized."

The state of Ohio had for a long time prior to the arrest of Dollree Mapp been asserting in case after case in their state courts that the Fourth Amendment did not apply to the states. Despite the fact that Ohio had their own state law requiring the issuing of search warrants, it was rarely observed.

It was against this backdrop that Ms. Mapp appealed her conviction. The Ohio State Court of Appeals upheld her conviction and the state's convenient interpretation of the Fourth Amendment. On further appeal, four out of the seven justices of the Ohio State Supreme Court found that the search by police and subsequent conviction were unconstitutional and voted to overturn the conviction. Unfortunately, Ohio State law requires that six out of seven justices must vote to overturn a law in order for it to be ruled unconstitutional. So by default, Dollree Mapp's conviction was upheld.

Despite not being a judge or legal scholar, Ms. Mapp strongly believed that Ohio was in fact still part of America and therefore had to come under the jurisdiction of the same United States Constitution as the rest of the country. So she appealed her case to the United States Supreme Court.

The Supreme Court heard *Mapp vs. Ohio* on March 29, 1961. The attorney representing Dollree Mapp was Alexander Kearns, and he was assisted by the American Civil Liberties Union.

Three months after hearing the case, the United States Supreme Court issued their ruling in *Mapp vs. Ohio*. The justices' five to three ruling found the search of Dollree Mapp's home unconstitutional due to violation of the Fourth Amendment's prohibition against unreasonable search and seizure, as well as the Fourteenth Amendment's guarantee of due process. "No state shall make or enforce any law which shall abridge the privileges or immunities of citizens of the United States nor shall any state deprive any person of life, liberty or property without due process of law."

In overturning the Mapp conviction, the court upheld the long-standing precedent of the "exclusionary rule," which prohibits the use of evidence in court obtained by an illegal search.

Writing for the Court, Justice Tom Clark stated, "The ignoble short-cut to conviction left open to the state tends to destroy the entire system of constitutional restraints on which the liberties of the people rest. Having once recognized that the right to privacy embodied in the Fourth Amendment is enforceable against the states and that the right to be secure against rude invasions of privacy by state officers is, there-fore constitutional in origin, we can no longer permit that right to remain an empty promise. Because it is enforceable in the same manner and to like effect as other basic rights secured by the Due Process Clause, we can no longer permit it to be revocable at the whim of any police officer that, in the name of law enforcement itself, chooses to sus-pend its enjoyment. Our decision, founded on reason and truth, gives to the individual no more than that which the Constitution guarantees him, to the police officer no less than that to which honest law enforce-ment is entitled and to the courts, that judicial integrity so necessary in the true administration of justice."

The *Mapp vs. Ohio* ruling of 1961 is one of the most frequently refer-enced landmark cases of constitutional law. But the concept of the Exclusionary Rule, which was at the core of that ruling, may no longer be in vogue decades later in America.

On February 7th, 1995, the United States House of Representatives passed House Resolution 666—the "Exclusionary Rule Reform Act"—by a vote of 303 to 121. That resolution for the first time in our history explicitly allowed prosecutors to use evidence in court that was illegally seized by police without a search warrant by virtue of what they termed a "good faith exception" to the Fourth Amendment.

In 1998, the American Bar Association published a report on constitutional rights and crime. After interviewing hundreds of judges, prosecutors, and police officers, the report concluded that the Exclusionary Rule neither causes serious malfunctioning of the criminal justice system nor promotes crime." The report went on to state "the police, toward whom the deterrent force of the Exclusionary Rule is primarily directed, do not consider search and seizure proscriptions to be a serious obstacle."

As far back as 1914, the Supreme Court stated in *Weeks vs. U.S.* that the Exclusionary Rule "is to deter [police misconduct]…to compel respect for the constitutional guarantee in the only effectively available way—by removing the incentive to disregard it."

Historically, the Exclusionary Rule compelled police departments throughout the country to conform to higher professional standards with regards to obtaining warrants, collecting evidence, and preparing cases. Arrests that were previously clouded by suspicion, illegality, and recklessness gave way to more efficient prosecutions resulting in higher conviction rates and less overturned convictions on appeal.

Ultimately, the "good faith exception" can only serve to encourage warrantless searches and seizures that for all intents and purposes will render the Fourth Amendment virtually meaningless. Police will increasingly be tempted to circumvent the warrant process and simply testify later that they erred "in good faith."

# VIII

---

## The Right to Counsel, Except in Florida

*"The rights of every man are diminished when the rights of any man is threatened."*

—*John F. Kennedy*

Clarence Gideon was born in Hannibal, Missouri, on August 30, 1910 to Charles and Virginia Gideon. His father died when he was three and his mother remarried a few years later to a man who has been described as a religious zealot and strict disciplinarian. Clarence Gideon did not get along well with his stepfather and ran away from home when he was thirteen.

During that cold winter of 1924, Gideon broke into a clothing store after hours and stole clothes to keep from freezing. The police tracked him down within hours and arrested him while still wearing the stolen items. He was subsequently tried and convicted of burglary and sentenced to three years in the state reform school. This conviction would mark the beginning of a long life of petty crimes that would find Gideon in and out of prison for the next forty years. Each time he was released he would make an attempt at earning an honest living, but would always end up running afoul of the law and sent back to prison.

After his release from the Texas State Penitentiary for burglary in 1952, Gideon moved to Florida. He took a job stocking and cleaning at the Bay Harbor Pool Room in Panama City, Florida. Soon thereafter, he was offered an opportunity to augment his meager income as a card dealer for gamblers in the back room. These games were supposedly protected from raids by a Panama City deputy sheriff who was running the games.

On June 2, 1961, Gideon was again arrested, this time charged with burglarizing the pool hall where he worked. Police on routine patrol in the early morning hours had discovered the door to the poolroom ajar. Upon further investigation, the officers found the vending machines inside had been broken into and the cash boxes emptied. Because of his police record, Gideon immediately became the prime suspect. Gideon professed his innocence and claimed he was being victimized because of his past. He cited the fact that with the keys to the poolroom in his possession, he would not have had to break in.

When his trial came up on August 4, 1961, he requested that presiding Judge Robert McCrary appoint counsel to represent him in the upcoming trial since he could not afford it on his own. But to his surprise, the judge denied his request outright, stating "Mr. Gideon, I am sorry, but I cannot appoint counsel to represent you in this case. Under the laws of the state of Florida, the only time the court can appoint counsel to represent a defendant is when that person is charged with a capital offense."

Gideon protested, though inaccurately, saying that, "The Supreme Court of the United States says I am entitled to be represented by counsel." What Gideon was actually recalling was the right to counsel provision of the Sixth Amendment to the United States Constitution.

The right-to-counsel clause has existed in the Bill of Rights since the beginning of the republic and most people of average intelligence would interpret it to mean exactly what it said. But, the spirit and intent of that right had somehow gotten lost in the process of a previous Supreme Court decision known as *Betts vs. Brady.* In that case, a man named Smith Betts was arrested and charged with robbery in Maryland. Just like Gideon, he also requested the judge appoint counsel to him since he could not afford it himself. The judge in that case also refused on the grounds that Maryland state law required that counsel only be appointed in cases of rape or murder. Betts appealed his case all the way up to the United States Supreme Court. In 1941, the high court decided in a six-to-three ruling that, in spite of what the Sixth Amendment said, a professional lawyer was not an absolute necessity to getting a fair trial. The Court held that a person of average intelligence was capable of properly defending himself in most court cases. The Court, however, did cite some possible exceptions to this rule which they called "special considerations," where counsel might be necessary, for example, if a defendant was illiterate, mentally incompetent, too young or if the case was too complicated for the defendant to comprehend.

Judge McCrary, aware of the *Betts vs. Brady* ruling and believing Gideon to be of average intelligence, persisted in turning down his request. At that point, Clarence Gideon had no choice in the matter, but to defend himself as best he could on his own. The outcome, quite predictably, was a guilty verdict with a sentence of five years in prison.

Clarence Gideon may have been an uneducated pauper and two-time loser but he had a virtue that many people do not—persistence. He believed he had a right to legal counsel and was not willing to take "no" for an answer. From his prison cell, he penciled a letter to the Florida State Supreme Court, citing the fact that he was denied his constitutional right to legal representation during his trial and that this had resulted in his conviction. Any such letter, which protests being held under illegal pretenses, is called in legal jargon a "writ of habeas corpus."

The Florida Supreme Court reviewed his case on October 30, 1961, and ruled in favor of honoring Florida state law regarding counsel over that of the United States Constitution, thus upholding Gideon's conviction.

But still Gideon did not give up. He continued to appeal his conviction to the United States Supreme Court. Upon arrival at the large, marble building all petitions seeking review of their case are filed into one of two main categories. Those having the ability to pay the $100 filing fee and other legal and administration expenses incurred are filed under the "Appellate" category, while those that cannot afford to pay are filed under the "Miscellaneous" category and are designated "forma pauperis," meaning to proceed in the manner of a pauper. The only requirement for filing a pauperis petition is that the filer must submit an affidavit stating that they are unable to pay.

Tens of thousands of petitions requesting review of their case come to the United States Supreme Court each year. But only a few hundred of those cases are granted review by the court. The court makes this decision based on widespread ramifications of the case and not just the benefit of one litigant.

On most Fridays during the October-to-June term, the justices hold their weekly conference. This conference is held in the ornate conference room located in the rear of the Supreme Court building. Prior to the beginning of the conference each justice shakes the hand of all of the others, a total of 36 handshakes in all. They then take their seats at the large conference table with the newest justice appointed to the court sitting closest to the door. Since no one except the nine justices are permitted to be present in the room during the conference, should any messages arrive, the newest justice will answer the door to receive it. It is in this conference room that the justices argue and vote on the cases before them. It is also here that they decide which cases to review. Four of the nine justices must vote in favor of a case for review to be granted. All of these proceedings are strictly confidential, with no record being kept of what is said in the conference.

When a case is decided, one justice voting in the majority is selected to write the court's opinion. Each justice voting in the majority may then append their own opinion, should their reasons differ. In the case of dissenting justices, one is chosen among them to write the dissenting opinion. After these opinions are written, reviewed, and printed, they are released to the public along with the final vote, usually on Mondays.

The Court announced their decision to review the case designated *Gideon vs. Wainwright, Director of Department of Corrections for Florida* on June 4, 1962. The court selects an attorney randomly to plead a pauper's case. These lawyers are not compensated except for travel expenses to and from Washington. But an offer to argue a case before the United States Supreme Court is considered an honor and is rarely turned down.

The Supreme Court in this case choose Washington D.C. lawyer Abe Fortas, a partner in the law firm of Arnold, Fortas and Porter. Abe Fortas was an experienced and seasoned lawyer who had previous experience arguing before the Supreme Court. Just a few short years later, President Johnson would appoint Fortas a Justice of the Supreme Court himself.

As soon as he was advised of the attorney who would represent him in the review of his case, Clarence Gideon wrote Abe Fortas to give him some background information. He wrote that denying counsel to people who could not afford it was a common practice in Florida and that the Raiford State Prison was full of its victims. He also said he had personally witnessed one trial before and another immediately after his own where both defendants were denied counsel. Each trial was completed in about one hour with both jury's returning a guilty verdict after just fifteen minutes of deliberations. Gideon then asked rhetorically, is this justice?

With regards to his own case, Gideon said that he thought the charges against him were the results of a setup perpetrated by the Panama City deputy sheriff, who ran the card games, possibly because of a disagreement Gideon had had with him. Gideon closed with an apparent sense of destiny saying that, "I believe each era finds an improvement in law. Each year brings something new for the benefit of mankind. Maybe this will be one of those small steps forward."

After reviewing the transcripts of the trial, Fortas thought that Gideon had done a good job representing himself for a layman. But Fortas was convinced that a lawyer would have done better and possibly even won the case. Gideon had allowed inappropriate testimony, which was damaging to his case, to go unchallenged. He did not cross-examine questionable witnesses aggressively enough and basically missed many opportunities that could have dramatically helped his case. Fortas also said, "I am convinced that this judge in Panama City, Florida, tried to help Gideon defend himself, he just did it badly, as any judge would; it's not a judge's role to be a defense counsel."

The Florida Attorney General chose a young assistant named Bruce Jacob to plead the state's case before the Supreme Court. This of course is an experience that every young attorney dreams of. However, Jacob was seriously handicapped by the fact that his entire career at this point consisted of just three years of practice. Whether the state attorney general was doing Jacob a favor or was just prepared to write the case off as a lost cause is unknown. But never in the history of the Supreme Court was there such a mismatch of counsel as there was in this case. Jacob was further handicapped by the fact that the entire preparation for his case would largely be done by himself, unlike Fortas,' who enjoyed the full support of his entire law firm.

A suggestion made by one of the other assistants to the Florida Attorney General, who Jacob had decided to employ, was writing to the attorney generals of the other 49 states requesting that they submit amicus curiae (friend of the courts) briefs to the Supreme Court defending the states' rights to run their criminal justice system their own way, without undue interference from the federal government.

Half of the states did file amicus briefs, but much to the surprise of Jacob, most of those states filed briefs in favor of overturning *Betts vs. Brady*. One state that filed such a brief was Minnesota, whose Attorney General Walter F. Mondale wrote, "I believe in federalism and states' rights too, but I also believe in the Bill of Rights. Nobody knows better than an Attorney General or a prosecuting attorney that in this day and age furnishing an attorney to those who cannot afford to hire one is fair and feasible. Nobody knows better than we do that rules of criminal law and proceedings which baffle trained professionals can only overwhelm the uninitiated."

Shortly after Mondale filed his brief, Massachusetts Attorney General Edward McCormack wrote a brief, which the attorney generals from 21 other states signed. The fact that twenty-three states were in effect requesting that the United States Supreme Court mandate their criminal justice system was an unprecedented event.

The collective brief stated in part, "That in the world of today a man may be condemned to penal servitude for lack of means to supply counsel for his defense is unthinkable. We respectfully urge the conviction below be reversed. That *Betts vs. Brady* be reconsidered and that this court require that all persons tried for a felony in a states' court shall have the right to counsel as a matter of due process of the law and equal protection of the law." Only Alabama and North Carolina filed amicus briefs in favor of retaining the *Betts vs. Brady* decision.

The Supreme Court heard the arguments on the Gideon case on January 15, 1963. Each side is allotted one hour to state their case, with the side originally filing the grievance going first, followed by the respondent. Unlike a jury type trial, the justices ask the attorney's questions during the proceedings.

Abe Fortas stated his case by saying that twenty years of the *Betts* ruling has proven it is not practical as a rule of law, adding that it was in fact responsible for more appeals being filed than if it were a standard practice to provide counsel to indigents throughout the United States.

To further emphasize the point he said, "I hope I may be forgiven for saying that my heart was full of compassion for the judges having to review those records and look for special circumstances." He then asked, "How can a judge, when a man is arraigned, look at him and say there are special circumstances? Does the judge say, 'you look stupid' or 'your case involves complicated facts?'" Fortas then stated that he thought this concept was administratively unworkable.

Fortas also cited the fact that thirty-seven states now provided counsel for the poor in all felony trials and pointed to the extraordinary act of twenty-three states filing amicus briefs in favor of reversing *Betts*, including two which did not currently have provisions for providing counsel. He then concluded by saying that he thought all of this made a reversal of *Betts* necessary.

Surprisingly, Fortas said very little of the most obvious point of the case, the much-believed premise that the Fourteenth Amendment made all fundamental rights contained within the Bill of Rights applicable to the states. The Supreme Court of 1941, which ruled on *Betts vs. Brady,* disagreed. That Court did not hold counsel to be fundamental to a fair trial. Fortas knew that most of the present justices disagreed with the *Betts* ruling, but he also knew that it was a bone of contention among a couple of the more conservative justices. And he felt that it was such an obvious point that he could afford to leave it to the justices to draw their own conclusions.

After Fortas' hour was up, it was Bruce Jacobs turn. Jacob wasted no time jumping right into the very issue that Fortas so carefully avoided, arguing that the Sixth Amendment's guarantee of counsel to all who could not afford it did not apply to the states by absorption of the Fourteenth Amendment. Making that statement brought the wrath of the justices down on him as they aggressively queried and challenged him on that particular point.

Jacobs also predictably argued that the states ought to be left alone to administer their criminal justice system the way they saw fit, without interference on the part of the federal government. He pointed out that if all the states had to provide legal counsel for anyone who could not afford it, it would also require states to provide counsel for misdemeanors and traffic violations, which would bankrupt the states. And he warned that, "If *Betts* should be overruled by this court in the instant case, as many as 5,093 hardened criminals may be eligible to be released in one mass exodus in Florida alone, not to mention those in other states." He then requested that if the Supreme Court did overturn *Betts* that they not make it retroactive.

On March 18, 1963, the United States Supreme Court voted unanimously to overturn Gideon's conviction and to reverse the *Betts vs. Brady* decision of twenty years earlier. Justice Black wrote for the Court. "Upon full consideration we conclude that *Betts vs. Brady* should be overruled. In all cases the accused shall enjoy the right…to have the assistance of counsel for his defense.

"We construe this to mean that in federal courts counsel must be provided for defendants unable to employ counsel unless the right is competently and intelligently waived. The constraint laid by the (Sixth) Amendment upon the national courts expresses a rule so essential to a fair trial and so to, to due process of law, that it is made obligatory upon the states by the Fourteenth Amendment. We think the Court in *Betts* was wrong….in concluding that the Sixth Amendment's guarantee of counsel is not one of the fundamental rights."

Justice Black then cited half a dozen other rulings prior to the *Betts* decision where the right to counsel in state courts was upheld. "The fact is that in deciding as it did—that appointment of counsel is not a fundamental right, essential to a fair trial—the Court in *Betts vs. Brady* made an abrupt break with its own precedents. In returning to these old precedents, sounder we believe than the new, we but restore constitutional principles established to achieve a fair system of justice. Not only these precedents but also reason and reflection require us to recognize that in our adversary system of criminal justice, any person hauled into court, who is too poor to hire a lawyer, cannot be assured a fair trial unless counsel is provided for him. This seems to us to be an obvious truth, Governments, both state and federal, quite properly spend vast sums of money to establish machinery to try defendants accused of crime. Lawyers to prosecute are everywhere deemed essential to protect the public's interest in an orderly society. Similarly, there are few defendants charged with a crime, few indeed, who fail to hire the best lawyers they can get to prepare and present their defenses."

"Even the intelligent and educated layman has small and sometimes no skill in the science of law. If charged with crime, he is incapable, generally, of determining for himself whether the indictment is good or poor. He is unfamiliar with the rules of evidence. Left without the aid of counsel he may be put on trial without a proper charge, and convicted upon incompetent evidence, or evidence irrelevant to the issue or otherwise inadmissible. He lacks the skill and knowledge to adequately prepare his defense, even though he has a perfect one. He requires the guiding hand of counsel at every step in the proceedings against him. Without it, though he be not guilty, he faces the danger of conviction because he does not know how to establish his innocence."

After two years in prison, Gideon was finally re-tried in the same court and with the same judge, Robert McCrary, as before, but this time with legal counsel. On August 5, 1963, after just one-hour deliberation by the jury, Gideon was found not guilty and released.

The Gideon case is a good example of what it all too frequently takes to preserve our constitutional rights. You must not only know your rights and be willing to fight any attempt to deny them to you, but you must also have faith in what you believe those rights mean. The Bill of Rights was not designed for the benefit of lawyers or judges; it was designed for the protection of the people.

If you or I were to put forth a question of constitutional rights to a judge, considered to be among the most knowledgeable men on that subject, then regardless of how obvious the answer might be to us, the judge can still profess the opposite, and we would most likely assume he was right and we were wrong. But we would do well to keep in mind that our judicial system up to and very much including the United States Supreme Court is made up of human beings, who are just as prone to human error as any of us. And judges and justices alike do not exist in a vacuum. They all have their own political and social philosophies and prejudices. And history has proven they can be and frequently have been dead wrong.

If you think a wrong has been committed, an injustice done or a short cut taken, you are probably right and should trust your instincts. As in most instances, when our freedoms have been challenged from within, the last great guardian of that freedom has most frequently not been the president or the courts or the Congress, it has been the common man unwilling to be gagged or shackled by the intellectually ignorant.

# IX

---

# The Great Communist Witch Hunt

*"Why doesn't everybody leave everybody else the hell alone?"*

—*Jimmy Durante*

Machiavellianism is a philosophy, which denies the relevance of morality in politics, where acquisition of power is the ends by which any means necessary to acquire it is justified. There is probably no finer example of this philosophy being put into practice in American politics than the communist witch-hunts perpetrated by Senator Joseph R. McCarthy in the early 1950's.

Joe McCarthy had two goals in life; first to become a United States Senator, then a Supreme Court Justice. He first ran for the Senate in 1944, while still serving as an intelligence officer in the Pacific with the Marines' Dive Bomber Squadron 235. Contrary to popular belief, he never was a tail gunner. He lost his first bid for the Senate, but did very well for a candidate campaigning from half a world away.

In 1946, with the war over and McCarthy back in his home state of Wisconsin, he ran again as a conservative. His timing proved perfect as the political pendulum was beginning to swing to the right after nearly two decades of New Deal liberalism. He ran a brilliant and aggressive campaign, upsetting Senator Robert LaFollette Jr., a progressive Republican in the primary election. With that momentum behind him, he went on to a somewhat anti-climatic victory over his Democratic opponent in the general election.

On the world stage, with the Second World War barely over, a new menace appeared almost instantly to fill the void of evil left by the defeat of fascism. The new threat was communism. Premier Joseph Stalin of communist Russia was a brutal dictator believed at the time to be only slightly better than Hitler.

In 1944, the allied powers met in Pottsdam, Germany, to plan the post-war administration of the soon to be conquered enemy territory. Under the terms of the Pottsdam Conference, all enemy territory in Europe and Asia was to be divided up amongst the Allies. The understanding being that this occupation would be for the purpose of accepting the surrender of the enemy forces and administering an interim government until a new civilian government could be democratically elected. But it was quickly becoming evident that Russia was reneging on that promise and was instead intent on permanently annexing all of the territory under their jurisdiction. In stark contrast to the Russian imperialism, America wanted nothing more than to disengage their troops and go home. Communist Russia with its hypertrophied military was poised to move swiftly to fill any resultant void.

The war had left most of Europe decimated. Europe's entire infrastructure as well as its economies was in ruins. This situation provided fertile ground for exploitation. Russian military forces quickly moved into any territory in which there was no risk of significant armed resistance and supported surrogates where there was.

However, the so-called "Red Menace" was not contained to just Europe. In October 1949, Mao Tse-tung's communist army swept the nationalists Chinese under General Chaing Kai-shek from the mainland and out to the coastal island of Formosa.

Winston Churchill gave voice to the dangerous new world situation in a speech at Westminster College in Missouri, saying that an iron curtain had descended across Europe. Here in the United States, there was a great deal of anxiety concerning espionage. Whittaker Chambers admitted he had spied for the new Soviet Union and implicated Alger Hiss, a state department employee as also being a communist spy. Hiss denied these allegations to the grand jury but was indicted. His first trial resulted in a hung jury. He was found guilty of perjury in his second trail and sentenced to 5 years in prison. Also indicted were Julius and Ethel Rosenberg, who were found guilty and sentenced to death for selling nuclear secrets to Russia. Fear of world Soviet domination was running high in this country and some in Washington were advocating a pre-emptive nuclear strike against Russia while we still held a nuclear monopoly.

In the realm of American politics, there were many Republicans who were willing to exploit any angle that might help them recapture the White House after two decades of Democratic occupancy. The volatile, post-war situation gave them the perfect issue to exploit. They were quick to label the Pottsdam Conference a sell out to Russia and accused President Truman and the Democratic Party of being soft on communism. They further argued that all of the country's current domestic problems were the result of the New Deal, which they labeled as being an American experiment in socialism. And many people seemed to quickly forget how much these programs helped them when they needed it the most.

Under mounting pressure, President Truman appointed a commission authorized to investigate federal employees deemed to be in sensitive positions to determine if there was in fact any communists infiltrating the American system of government. Truman's investigation found no spies, but 80 federal employees were re-assigned anyway due to tightened security.

One night while Senator Joseph McCarthy was dining with a friend, who was a professor of political science at Georgetown University, the conversation turned to the politics of necessity. Namely what issue McCarthy could use to help him stand out from the other senators and assure his re-election in 1952. The professor suggested McCarthy become the point man against communist insurrection in this country. McCarthy realized how well invoking the communist bogeyman was already playing throughout the country and decided to expand upon it.

So armed with political necessity alone, McCarthy at that time proclaimed, "The Government is full of communists." He convinced himself and would now commence convincing America of the great Red Menace within. And so it was that the great American nightmare, which would eventually come to known as McCarthyism, began. Before it was over, more than 4 million people would end up being investigated. Thousands of people would be subpoenaed to appear at various hearings. Many would lose or be denied jobs just over the stigma attached to being questioned.

McCarthy didn't invent invoking the communist bogeyman, many politicians at this time were hunting communists, but no one used the issue more extensively or effectively, offering up specific numbers of communist spies if not names or evidence.

McCarthy kicked off his campaign of fear in Wheeling, West Virginia, on February 9, 1950. It was there he made an impassioned speech warning that "the final battle between communism and Christianity" had begun. He blamed our impotency in fighting it as being due to the "traitorous actions" of some of our own countrymen working in the U.S. State Department. He then added, "While I do not have the time to name all the men in the State Department who had been named as active members in a communist spy ring, I have here in my hand a list of 205 names…that were made known to the Secretary of State…and who are still working in the State Department."

McCarthy spent the next several weeks crisscrossing the country making the same baseless accusations, never divulging a single name. The numbers of "communists spies" varied widely from place to place and from time to time. But the result was always the same; people believed him and were left scared.

The State Department contacted McCarthy asking for any names he might have and promising swift action. McCarthy responded directly to the president, stating that the records were not presently available to him, but he knew of 300 names that had been provided to the Secretary of State of which only 80 had been discharged, referring to the 80 that were reassigned under Truman's internal investigation. President Truman knew a farce when he saw one and publicly denied McCarthy's charges.

In addition to the silent acquiesce of many of his colleagues in Congress, McCarthy also enjoyed the support and advice from many in the Republican leadership. Senator John Bircher told McCarthy, "Joe you're a dirty son of a bitch, but there are times when you've got to have a son of a bitch around and this is one of those times." Senator Taft advised McCarthy, "If one case doesn't work, try another."

On February 20, 1950, he stood on the floor of the United States Senate, waving a hand full of papers claiming to have, "pierced Truman's iron curtain of secrecy" and claiming to have the names of 81 communist spies still working in the State Department. Many senators requested he be more specific with his allegations, so he proceeded to refer to specific case numbers followed by a long and rambling synopsis. He talked in circles and by the time he was done, everyone was thoroughly confused. He concluded by saying that he had no desire to hide behind his Senate immunity and that if his accusations proved to be false he would resign from the Senate. Then he ended by requesting that public hearings be held where he would name names. At this point, congressmen opposed to McCarthy were willing to just sit back, let him play out his game and self-destruct, not fully appreciating the probability that he would destroy the lives of many innocent people before that happened.

His accusations were reported verbatim in the news and went largely unchallenged by the press or his colleagues. Based on the one-sided story most people were hearing, who among the public would doubt him? Never in the history of the United States had there been a person in such a high and trusted position as a United States Senator, who lied on such a grand scale.

The Senate created a committee to investigate McCarthy's charges and appointed Maryland Senator Millard Tydings as chairman, but it would be McCarthy who would dominate the proceedings.

The hearings began on March 8, 1950, in the Senate caucus room, which was filled to capacity with newsmen. Using the very list provided to the Senate by the State Department containing the names of those 80 government workers who had already been re-assigned, McCarthy simply embellished the cases. As was his style throughout this entire charade, he would avoid specifics, constantly alluding to classified files. He basically placed the burden of proving innocence upon the accused. This was a deceitful, but effective tactic that succeeded quite well in the quasi-law environment of a Senate committee hearing contrary to any proper court of law where it would have quickly been thrown out.

With the popular belief that the nuclear sword of Damocles was hanging over America's head, most people did not feel that we could afford the convenience of civil liberties or fairness. Nor was it a time for decorum or details. The mad rush was on to do whatever had to be done to purge ourselves of the Red Menace from within.

Most congressional Republicans jumped on the bandwagon and exploited the issue for all it was worth, intentionally fanning the fires of fear. Many people started to believe there was a communist hiding under every bed and in every closet in America. No one was above suspicion. Federal, state, and even local governments instituted loyalty oaths for teachers and many other public employees, who were not even remotely involved with positions of national security. Many citizens groups joined in the paranoia and the American Legion lead the way, once more offering their amateur spying services to the FBI.

For the next four months, McCarthy held the country on the edge of their seats with these hearings. J. Edgar Hoovers' FBI was secretly providing McCarthy with classified information. But all of this information was based on the weakest and most circumstantial evidence and innuendo, provided by all sorts of cranks, crackpots, and pranksters. Those targeted were people the FBI could not build a legitimate legal case against, but whom Hoover felt deserved to at least be harassed. McCarthy bragged about his American Underground; government workers and military personnel who were by-passing the chain of command they had sworn to obey and passing classified information directly to him.

On Friday March 10, McCarthy stated that he would name the top Soviet spy in the U.S. the following Monday. The country held their breath over the weekend. When Monday finally came, McCarthy accused Owen Lattimore as the Soviet's Mr. Big in the United States. Lattimore was a political science professor at John Hopkins University and an authority on the Orient who had advised Presidents Roosevelt and Truman on foreign policy in the Pacific.

At the time of this announcement, Lattimore was out of the country, but upon being informed of the accusation being leveled against him, he immediately returned home. The committee requested all files on Lattimore from the FBI be turned over to them. Hoover refused, but did permit the committee to view them at FBI headquarters. All members of the committee except for McCarthy went to FBI headquarters for the private viewing. McCarthy at this point stated that he had better information than the FBI.

On April 6, 1950, Owen Lattimore appeared before the committee and officially denied ever having any connections with the Communist Party. Senator Tydings stated that the committee had reviewed the FBI files on Mr. Lattimore and found nothing that linked him to the Communist Party or any spy ring and thanked him for his cooperation. McCarthy responded by accusing his own committee of lying about Lattimore.

Undaunted, McCarthy moved on and continued with his speeches and press releases. By this time, McCarthy had acquired so much power in the court of public opinion that no one dared to challenge him for fear that they too would be accused of being a communist. But one courageous Republican senator, Margaret Chase Smith of Maine, took the lead no one else would in condemning his tactics on the Senate floor, stating, "I think it is high time that we remember that we have sworn to uphold and defend the Constitution. I think it is high time that we remember that the Constitution, as amended, speaks of trial by jury instead of jury by accusation. Those of us who shout the loudest about Americanism in making character assassinations are all too frequently those who, by our own words and acts, ignore some of the basic principles of Americanism—The right to criticize, the right to hold unpopular beliefs, the right to protest, the right of independent thought.

"The exercise of these rights should not cost one single American citizen his reputation, or his right to a livelihood nor should he be in danger of losing his reputation or livelihood merely because he happens to know someone who holds unpopular beliefs. Who of us does not?"

Unfortunately, Senator Smith's "declaration of conscience" speech as it would come to be known failed to rally any significant support and the witch-hunt continued.

McCarthy was forever promising to provide the hard evidence to verify his accusations, but what he ended up revealing was always far less. And by making so many accusations at such a fast pace, a battalion of newsmen could not keep up with him. Just as Senator Taft had suggested, as soon as one accusation came close to losing credibility, he simply moved on to another.

By now McCarthy had become a power in his own right. Anyone who dared to criticize him was instantly labeled a communist or communist sympathizer and accused of trying to impede his investigation and hide the truth from the American people.

On June 25, 1950, the Cold War turned hot in Korea and President Truman chose to fight a limited "police action" in the hopes of preventing an all-out war with China or perhaps even a nuclear war with the Soviet Union. President Truman ordered General MacArthur to make no statements concerning this controversial strategy and negotiate no terms with the enemy unless first clearing the terms with the White House. When General MacArthur disobeyed these orders by releasing a series of statements contrary to official U.S. policy, Truman relieved MacArthur of his command.

Back on the home front, McCarthy accused the president of treason and stated that he should be impeached for firing MacArthur. Then he made the ridiculous insinuation that the president of United States was a closet communist.

On June 14, 1951 McCarthy accused Secretary of Defense General George Marshall of being a traitor and the defacto head of the pro-communist conspiracy within the United States government. Once tainted by McCarthy, George Marshall's long and honorable career of service to the country both in and out of uniform was destroyed.

As absurd as many of these charges were, most people saw a United States Senator making bold accusations that were too bazaar not be true. Except for those stung by his attack, no one challenged anything he said. Throughout the country, actors, writers, directors, and artists of all types were blacklisted by mere whispers of anti-patriotism, which frequently only meant holding some liberal political opinions.

The Tydings Committee finally concluded their investigation and issued their report calling McCarthy's crusade, "a fraud and a hoax perpetrated on the Senate of the United States and the American people." But still none of the leaders in Congress were willing to take the lead in stopping McCarthy. McCarthy condemned the report of his own committee as a "white wash," and then he retaliated by going into Maryland and actively campaigning against Tydings' bid for re-election.

McCarthy's coup against Tydings did not stop with just conventional campaigning, as he resorted to doctoring photographs of Tydings having what appeared to be a friendly chat with a well-known member of the Communist Party. Something that would have been too ridiculous to be believed at any other time, but in 1950, an accusation was as good as a conviction. Unfortunately, the people of Maryland and the rest of the country did not learn the truth of this matter until after the election. Being painted as a Communist sympathizer by McCarthy, Tydings lost the election.

McCarthy purposely appealed to the darker side of people, the side that harbors suspicion, fear, and hate. The paranoia he initiated quickly snowballed until the Red Scare reached epidemic proportions. Anyone with an ax to grind had only to start a rumor or give an anonymous tip. No proof was required and no innuendo was too frivolous. Anyone to the left of a conservative Democrat was painted as either a Communist Red, or if given the benefit of the doubt, a sympathetic Pink.

Many Conservative politicians followed McCarthy's lead. In the true spirit of anything goes to win an election, questioning peoples' patriotism became a national pastime. McCarthy became the Republican's hatchet man and was in great demand by campaign committees throughout the country.

By throwing his prestige behind an underdog candidate in Maryland and bringing a senior member of Congress down, McCarthy became even more feared and powerful. In fact, McCarthy has been credited with electing a dozen members to the Senate and helping Eisenhower win the White House. He assured the people throughout the campaign that if Eisenhower were elected, America would finally have a president who really would fight communism. However, as soon as the election was over, McCarthy who was by now drunk with power and wanting even more, turned his guns on his own party's president, though in somewhat muted tones.

The Republican leadership finally came to realize what an uncontrollable monster they had created. Shortly after Eisenhower's election, McCarthy claimed, "We've only scratched the surface of communism." He further claimed that his informants had advised him that the government's personnel records had been tampered with and damaging information concerning homosexuals and communists in the government had been expunged. It soon became apparent that he had no intention of stopping his witch-hunt.

There were ever-increasing grumbles in private, on both sides of the aisle of Congress and in the White House about McCarthy. Still they all feared to challenge him publicly. McCarthy was the most powerful politician in American and most of what was reported in the media made him look like the savior of America. At the height of the communist witch-hunt, the Chief Justice of the United States Supreme Court suggested that, "if the Bill of Rights were put to a vote today, it would lose."

In January 1953, the new Congress convened and the powerful senator from Wisconsin became the Chairman of the Subcommittee on Investigations of Government Operations. McCarthy promptly decided to convene hearings on communist infiltration in the U.S. Army. His increased power and responsibilities in the Senate required him to hire several staff members. Ironically, it would be two of his own staff members that would ultimately cause his downfall.

For his chief counsel, he chose a young attorney named Roy Cohn. He also hired David Shine as a special consultant on communism. Shine was a freelance journalist who specialized on communism, although much of what he wrote on the subject was later discovered to be grossly inaccurate.

For the next year, McCarthy would continue to accuse, criticize, and confound the legitimate government of the United States, to a large extent holding the president and Congress hostage to his whims. But a fateful chain of events would soon bring McCarthy's reign of terror to a screeching halt.

In July 1953, David Shine received his draft notice for service in the Army. McCarthy and Cohn tried, not all too subtly to pull strings to have Shine assigned as special assistant to the Secretary of the Army, Robert T. Stevens. The Army brass largely ignored these overtures. Shine attended boot camp at Fort Dix, New Jersey, where he was granted all kinds of special privileges unheard of for a recruit, regardless of their previous civilian status.

But still McCarthy was not satisfied. He put even more pressure on the Army brass up to and including the U.S. Army Secretary himself to get special duty for Shine. The Army continued to resist. Finally, Cohn in a fit of rage threatened an Army general that he would "wreck the Army," and alluded to security risks within the Army. This was a threat the Army brass did not ignore. Secretary Stevens released a report detailing the numerous attempts made by McCarthy and his staff to pull strings on behalf of Private Shine. McCarthy responded by accusing the Army of trying to use Shine as a pawn to buy him off further investigations of the Army.

After all the charges and counter charges flew between the Department of the Army and McCarthy, the showdown finally came when the Senate empanelled yet another committee to conduct hearings, which would come to be known as the Army-McCarthy hearings. The Army-McCarthy hearings would hold the country's rapt attention for five long weeks. The committee was composed of seven U.S. Senators, with Senator Karl Mundt of South Dakota presiding as chairman. The special committee was empowered to investigate all charges both sides had made.

The difference between this and other hearings was that this one would be conducted under the watchful eye of television and carried nationwide. So that for the first time the entire country would get to see how McCarthy operated using his political slight of hand.

The climax to the hearing came when the Army's counsel, Joe Welsh, was questioning Roy Cohn, asking why, if he had information of security risks in the Army and was so frequently and personally conferring with the U.S. Army Secretary, he did not opt to share this concern with him? Why did he not give the proper authorities the chance to do anything, but rather chose to short circuit the system?

Before Cohn could answer, McCarthy interrupted and dove into a long rambling tirade of how a man named Fred Fisher who he identified as a staff member of the investigation committee happened to be associated with a communist front organization. The chairman interrupted McCarthy to say that no such person was serving on his committee. McCarthy did not let this trivial detail slow him down one bit and continued his tirade.

Even Roy Cohn looked stunned as McCarthy continued his incoherent attack. Finally after several minutes, a disgusted Joseph Welsh admitted that he was considering using Mr. Fisher as part of his team, but Mr. Fisher had admitted to him that during his college days that he had been a member of the Lawyers Guild, which has since been branded as a communist front organization for its work in defending accused communists.

Joe Welsh then asked McCarthy why since he has been sitting just six feet from him throughout this entire hearing he could not have just privately asked him about Mr. Fisher if he was so concerned instead of publicly destroying his reputation on nationwide television? He then added, "Let us not assassinate this young lad any further, Senator, have you no decency Sir, at long last have you left no sense of decency?"

But still McCarthy would not stop his attack, trying to turn the investigation into a kangaroo court on someone who had nothing to do with the business at hand. Welsh let him dig himself in deeper for a good many more minutes, then finally stated he would not discuss Fred

Fisher with him further. The hearing room exploded with applause and McCarthy with a blank look on his face had no idea what it was all about. But America was finally awakening from their four-year nightmare of McCarthyism. McCarthy overplayed his hand and now looking confused asked, "What did I do?"

On June 17, 1954, the special committee on the Army-McCarthy investigation made public their report. And in the true spirit of partisan politics, all Republicans except for one found nothing inappropriate in McCarthy's actions, while all of the Democrats voted against him. Officially their report was non-conclusive, but television did what the politicians would not do. McCarthy was de-fanged, and the witch-hunt was over.

After all the hearings, after thousands of witnesses testifying and millions of investigations being conducted, not a single charge of espionage was filed nor a single spy discovered. But thousands of lives were disrupted or destroyed and the entire country left paralyzed with fear for the better part of four years.

Shortly after the Army-McCarthy hearings, a resolution was introduced on the floor of the Senate to censure Joe McCarthy for his reckless and dangerous actions. But when all was said and done, McCarthy never faced a single criminal charge, he never faced a single civil charge, he was not impeached from the Senate, and in a true display of the arrogance of power, the Senate even refused to censure him. For all of the damage Joseph McCarthy had reaped on this country, he paid only the *terrible* price of a written reprimand.

# X

---

# The Civil Rights Marathon

*"So long as we have enough people in this country willing to fight for their rights, we'll continue to be called a democracy."*

—*Roger Baldwin, Founder ACLU*

On January 1, 1863, in the midst of the American Civil War, President Abraham Lincoln issued one of the most virtuous documents in history, the Emancipation Proclamation, which by executive order freed all slaves in the United States. The war would rage on for two more years, but immediately after it was over, the Thirteenth Amendment would be passed, which ended slavery forever in the United States with the full force of the highest law of the land.

While the country may have been divided on the question of slavery, it proved to be less sympathetic to granting even the most basic civil rights to the slaves once they were freed. For this reason, Congress subsequently passed the Fourteenth and Fifteenth Amendments, which in effect granted full citizenship to the former slaves—at least on paper. In reality, they would remain in political and economic bondage for another hundred years.

Conservatives would fight the civil rights movement every step of the way. First by ridiculously arguing that the United States Constitution only applied to the federal government and not to the states within the union, then when that argument was finally lost, holding that businesses within the states did not come under the jurisdiction of either state or federal laws.

Not until the 1960's did the civil rights movement begin to take center stage in American politics. In part because the black man's patience had run out over rights denied for two-hundred years and also because for the first time in generations the country was not distracted by some sort of national emergency, domestic or foreign. It had been six years since the U.S. Supreme Court ruled for desegregation in the historic *Brown vs. Board of Education* case, yet only about one percent of the schools in the South were desegregated and no additional movement was in sight.

Over the years, various civil rights organizations were founded such as: the National Association for the Advancement of Colored People, the Congress for Racial Equality and the Southern Christian Leadership Conference, to name just a few. They were all about to come of age in the greatest civil rights campaign in history, which would take the form of sit-ins, marches, and freedom rides. This great crusade would begin during and majorly effect the presidential election of 1960.

Just as the 1960 presidential election started to heat up, so did the civil rights movement. On February 1, 1960, four black freshman students at Greensboro College in North Carolina entered the local Woolworths department store, sat at the "white only" lunch counter there and demanded service. This action was so radical at the time that the black waitress working there even admonished them saying, "Fellows like you make our race look bad" and refused to serve them. But they coolly announced that they would remain there until they were served.

Word of the sit-in spread quickly and hundreds of other students came from miles around to join the sit-in, keeping the vigil at the lunch counter in shifts. The students collectively occupied those seats until closing. And when the store re-opened the next morning, they were waiting at the door to re-occupy the seats. This sit-in quickly spurred similar sit-ins at other eating establishments in North Carolina and throughout the South.

Nothing much except sitting happened for the first few days, then on the third day arrests were made. But as soon as they were arrested, other students appeared to take their place. The students announced that if they were going to be arrested for standing up for their rights, they would fill up the jails of the South.

Once it became apparent that just ignoring the students would not dissuade them, the authorities opted for cracking down on them. At sit-ins in Nashville, police made arrests for loitering, trespassing, and disorderly conduct. Before making those arrests, however, the police allowed the white crowd to beat the demonstrators. After a few days of demonstrators being arrested, bailed out, and immediately returning to demonstrate, Mayor Ben Wade agreed to a truce. If students called off their sit-ins, he would release all prisoners and empanel a committee to hear their grievances.

But as would be the case with so many of their victories, it would be two steps forward and one step back. The price of even this modest victory would be a dramatic increase in unprovoked violent attacks against blacks. A Montgomery newspaper captured one such act of retaliation with a front-page picture of a white man hitting a black woman over the head with a baseball bat, while police just stood by and watched. Although the woman was knocked unconscious and suffered a severe concussion, no arrest was made despite the fact that the assailant was easily identifiable in thousands of newspapers.

The Democratic presidential candidate, Massachusetts Senator John F. Kennedy, was convinced by his experience in Congress that further advances in civil rights were not politically possible in the legislative branch and saw presidential leadership via executive orders as the best course of action. He accused the Republican administration of failing to provide leadership on the issue, saying that President Eisenhower had ignored many opportunities to improve the plight of the black man, which he had the power to do "with just the stroke of a pen." Kennedy insisted upon a strong civil rights platform in the Democratic Party's platform.

This proved to be not only good statesmanship but also good politics. His stand helped to barely push him over the top in three key states where the majority of blacks voted for him. Many historians have speculated that without that commitment to civil rights, which translated into black votes, he would not have won the election.

Little did Kennedy know how much his administration would be bogged down fighting for civil rights. There would be other problems for sure, but civil rights would consume more of his administration's time and energy than any other single issue. Each year would bring a new crisis that seemed to push the country to the brink of another civil war.

Shortly after assuming office, Attorney General Robert Kennedy emphasized the administration's commitment to civil rights in a speech at the University of Georgia. Referring to the Supreme Courts' recent decisions pertaining to desegregation, he stated that, "We will enforce the law in every field and every region…If orders of the Courts are circumvented, the Department of Justice will act".

No sooner had the attorney general spoken those words than he was confronted by his first civil rights crisis. CORE—the Congress for Racial Equality—dispatched groups of "Freedom Riders" on Trailways and Greyhound buses with the specific mission of violating segregation laws at bus terminals and restaurants throughout the South.

They got through Virginia and the Carolinas' largely unscathed, but then came Anniston, Alabama. It was there that the Greyhound bus was met by a white mob armed with pipes, clubs, bricks, and knives. As soon as the bus pulled in, the mob wasted no time in surrounding and attacking it. They shook the bus violently and taunted the passengers to come out. The bus driver promptly decided against a prolonged visit in Anniston and took off down the road. But the mob piled into to several waiting cars and pickup trucks and chased after them. The bus did not make it much father than a mile down the road before all of its tires went flat as a result of them being slashed back at the depot.

Once the mob caught up to the bus, the vigilantes began beating their clubs and pipes against the bus, breaking the windows and trying to pry the door open. The passengers, fearing for their lives, held the door shut. Then the mob torched the bus by throwing a Molotov cocktail in a window. As heavy black smoke began filling the bus and choking the passengers the tug of war at the bus door was reversed. The passengers tried desperately to open the door and escape while the mob held the door shut.

An undercover officer onboard the bus pulled out his pistol and drove the mob away from the door. The passengers burst through the door to relative safety, knowing that at least they would not be incinerated. A club hit the undercover officer from behind once he was clear of the bus, and the mob was soon swarming over all of the passengers, brutally beating them in the middle of the street. The state police showed up several minutes later and had the Freedom Riders taken to the hospital. But even the sanctity of the hospital offered little safety. Soon after the Freedom Riders arrival came a caravan of the Ku Klux Klan, demanding that the hospital turn the newly arrived patients over to them. The hospital refused and was able to stall them long enough for a caravan of gun-toting black men from a nearby church to show up and drive them off.

The second group of Freedom Riders on a Trailways bus was due to arrive in Birmingham about an hour after the Greyhound bus had arrived in Anniston. Under a prearranged agreement between Police Commissioner Bull Connors and the KKK, the Birmingham mob would be given 15 minutes to beat the Freedom Riders before the police would arrive to break it up.

Upon learning of this, the pastor from Bull Connors' church, the Reverend John Rutland, went to Connors' office and pleaded with him not to permit the beatings to take place. But the pastor's pleas fell on deaf ears; segregation in the South at the time was above both the law and religion.

When the Trailways bus arrived in Birmingham later that day, the Freedom Riders debarked the bus and headed for the "white only" lounge, running a gauntlet of Klansmen. Their path became narrower and more menacing as they proceeded. First there was threatening language, then pushing and shoving then it quickly degenerated into an all-out savage beating with a mob of a hundred swarming all over the eight defenseless Freedom Riders. As with any mob, the violence did not stay contained to just the original targets, reporters and photographers were also beaten and their cars and equipment smashed. Other people at the depot, both black and white, who knew nothing about the situation were attacked just on suspicion. As the mob broke up with the scheduled arrival of the police, they then proceeded to roam the city, stopping to beat any black person—man, woman or child they happened to come across on their way home.

Upon hearing of this, Attorney General Kennedy contacted Governor Patterson asking him to guarantee the Freedom Riders safe passage out of Alabama, but the governor vowed to uphold Alabama's segregation laws and refused to aid the "out of state rabble-rousers." As a result, the attorney general dispatched 600 federal marshals to escort them out of the hostile territory of Alabama. But even as the attorney general was negotiating for the safe return of the first group of Freedom Riders, CORE was dispatching a second group to pick up where the first had left off.

With the segregation battle heating up over the Freedom Riders, the Reverend Martin Luther King Jr. decided to go to Alabama to show his support. The attorney general advised him against the trip, but when

King proved adamant, 50 federal marshals were assigned to protect him.

King arrived at Reverend Ralph Abernathy's church in Montgomery, where some of the fugitive Freedom Riders were being hidden in the basement. Whether it was because of King's arrival or rumor of the Freedom Riders being hidden there, a large crowd of whites soon gathered and surrounded the church. The federal marshals assigned to protect King spread out around the church and held the crowd back. But the crowd grew larger and uglier by the minute.

The situation at the church was fast becoming critical and beyond the control of just 50 federal marshals. Not a single state or local policeman was in sight. As the congregation sang hymns inside the church, hateful taunts filled the air outside the church. The unruly crowd began throwing rocks and bottles at the church. Then after two hours of taunts and bottle throwing, the crowd began closing in on the church. The marshals on the scene fired their tear gas, dispersing the crowd temporarily. They then made a desperate call for reinforcements. Additional federal marshals were already being flown into nearby Maxwell Air Force Base from neighboring states.

The stained glass windows of the church were broken by rocks, and tear gas filled the church, but the parishioners had no place to run. The church was the only thing standing between them and the mob outside. In preparation for the impending siege of the church, the children were taken into the basement. The crowd was now ramming the church door. Then just like the cavalry in a Hollywood movie, the reinforcements finally arrived. They fired massive amounts of tear gas, adding to that which was already hanging in the air. The newly arrived marshals then wedged themselves between the church and the mob and began pushing the mob back.

The tear gas continued to break up the attacks, but the determined mob quickly regrouped and attacked again. Just as the attorney general was about to request army troops from Fort Benning, Georgia, Alabama

National Guardsmen arrived and dispersed the crowd with fixed bayonets. Upon his arrival, General Henry Graham announced that Governor Patterson had declared martial law throughout the city with a dusk-to-dawn curfew to take effect immediately.

The churchgoers' elation, however, was short-lived because when they went to leave the church to go home, the bayonets were then turned on them. A few disbelieving parishioners who tried to push their way through were pushed back with rifle butts and bayonets. In a very short period of time their church had gone from a safe haven to a prison. It had already been a long and stressful night for the parishioners and the discomfort was greatly increased by the unseasonably hot and humid weather and the remnants of tear gas hanging in the still night air.

Again the attorney general contacted the governor and intense negotiations ensued for another hour. Only after the attorney general threatened immediate federal intervention did the governor relent and in a bizarre turn of events agree to have the National Guardsmen transport the parishioners to their homes.

The Freedom Riders would stubbornly continue to travel throughout the South and meet with violence for months. But after the first Freedom Riders forced the showdown between Alabama and the federal government, local police were much quicker to assume their proper roles as protectors of civil order, if only to prevent federal intervention. As time marched on, the journeys of the Freedom Riders became less news and more routine.

Both President Kennedy and Dr. Martin Luther King were committed to sweeping changes in civil rights, but they came from two distinctly different backgrounds and therefore held two entirely different philosophies on how best to pursue it. Kennedy was the pragmatic politician and was looking more for what was doable by following the path of least resistance. King on the other hand, was a crusader who had experienced racial oppression first hand and was convinced that change would only come about if forced upon those who were resistant to it.

King and Kennedy disagreed over how fast civil rights should be pushed. King did not hesitate to publicly criticize the president for his "slow, cautious pace," but was just as quick to admit that no administration had done more for civil rights. The one issue they both gave top priority to, however, was extending voting rights, because if blacks could secure the right to vote, they would have more direct control over their own destinies. Elected officials would have no choice but to deal with them more fairly if they wanted to be re-elected.

Even as the furor over the Freedom Riders slowly dissipated, the next major civil rights crisis was forming. Air Force veteran James Meredith applied for admission to the University of Mississippi in 1961, but was turned down for no specific reason. Sensing that the fact that he was a black man applying to an all-white college might have something to do with it, he filed suit in U.S. District Court. The court initially sided with the university and dismissed the suit. But on appeal, a higher court ruled that Meredith was rejected solely on racial grounds and ordered his admittance.

Mississippi Governor Ross Barnett said in a paradoxical kind of statement "...we will not surrender to the evil and illegal forces of tyranny," and so began the next civil rights battle between the Kennedy administration and the southern states of America.

On September 20, 1962, James Meredith arrived to register on campus with an escort of several federal marshals. Governor Barnett met Meredith and the marshals by personally blocking the door to the admissions building. Three attempts were made by the federal marshals, each time re-appearing with a new court order in hand, which of course is meaningless to those having no respect for the law, unless of course there is sufficient force to compel the law's enforcement. Each time they returned to register, the same unrepentant governor and an ever-increasing mob of whites met them.

Over the next two weeks the situation escalated dramatically. The Kennedy administration finally moved a sufficient number of troops to force the registration, but by then there were thousands of armed vigilantes from across the state that had converged on the campus. President Kennedy nationalized the Mississippi National Guard. The National Guard and the U.S. Army troops that had been dispatched there were poised to enforce the court order. But it had become apparent that to do so would provoke a major battle with a great number of casualties being imminent. Because of this concern, the administration decided to pull back. Governor Barnett by now also began to realize what an explosive situation he had created and agreed to register Meredith in the state capital, away from the potential battle ground of the university.

This last battle of wills over segregation was won, but again at a price. Racially motivated attacks greatly increased after Meredith's admission. For the next four years, James Meredith went through the daily routine of obtaining a college education, but was constantly surrounded by federal marshals and continually being accosted, verbally threatened, spat upon and occasionally assaulted.

In June 1963, another episode similar to the Meredith registration was played out all over again, this time at the University of Alabama, when two blacks tried to enroll. Alabama Governor George Wallace mimicked the act of Governor Barnett by physically blocking the entrance to that university's registration building. Again the National Guard was nationalized. This time things moved a little more quickly and smoothly. Wallace apparently only wished to play up to the crowd and backed down as soon as confronted by a National Guard colonel who presented him with a court order to register the applicants.

Ironically this civil right confrontation took place during the 100th anniversary of the Emancipation Proclamation, which only served to underscore how little real progress had been made on civil rights even after a terrible civil war had been fought and a century had passed.

On June 13, 1963, President Kennedy felt compelled to point this out to the American people. In a nationwide TV address on civil rights, he proclaimed that, "This is a moral issue as old as the scriptures and as clear as the Constitution. A great chance is at hand and our task, our obligation is to make this revolution, this change, peaceful and constructive for all." He then challenged Congress to pass sweeping civil rights legislation including authorization to withhold federal funds from any state that practices segregation. But even as the president appealed to the nation's conscience, the director of the Mississippi branch of the NAACP—Medgar Evers—was gunned down in front of his home in Jackson, Mississippi.

On August 28, 1963, a quarter of a million people from across the United States marched on Washington in a peaceful demonstration. The culmination of that march was a rally at the Lincoln Memorial, where Martin Luther King Jr. made his historic and moving "I Have a Dream" speech.

But civil rights demonstrations any further South than the nation's capital continued to be anything but peaceful. In Birmingham, Alabama, Bull Connors continued to approve of and even incite violence against blacks. As a result, white mobs burned the homes of blacks and attacked civil rights demonstrators with chains and clubs while the authorities used fire hoses and dogs, and then arrested the demonstrators for disorderly conduct. In September 1963, these vicious attacks reached an all-time low when four young girls were killed in the bombing of a black church in Birmingham, Alabama.

The Civil Rights Commission appointed by President Kennedy reported that, "Citizens of the United States have been shot, set upon by vicious dogs, beaten, and otherwise terrorized because they sought to vote. Since October, students have been fired upon, ministers have been assaulted…children, at the brink of starvation have been deprived of assistance by the callous and discriminatory acts of Mississippi officials administering federal funds." The commission unanimously agreed that only further steps by the federal government could arrest the sub-version of the Constitution in the South.

President Kennedy suggested to the committee that they not release the report, saying the report was too harsh and that it would alienate moderate Southern congressmen that were needed to pass any civil rights legislation, but he conceded that the final decision was the committee's to make and he would not attempt to suppress it. It was released.

In spite of the committee's recommendation, there was a great deal of debate over the authority of the federal government to take action on any pending civil rights cases. These cases first had to work their way up through the state and lower federal courts. In reality, the odds of any such cases making it that far were small, given the fact that these courts were so heavily stacked against any such progressive movement in civil rights. Also, Attorney General Bobby Kennedy knew full well that the justice department did not have the resources to occupy all of the rebellious southern states in order to compel them to adhere to the desegregation and voters' rights laws. To do that would require a significant portion of the United States military and could conceivably incite another civil war.

On November 22, 1963, President Kennedy was assassinated in Dallas, Texas, and the civil rights baton and the presidency were passed to Vice President Lyndon Johnson. On civil rights, President Kennedy was a profile in courage, but probably lacked the political clout in Congress to get any significant civil rights legislation passed. It probably took the unique combination of having a southern, consummate wheeler-dealer type-like Lyndon Johnson, also acting in the name of the martyred president, for him to have succeeded. If all of these tragic and fateful things had not fallen into place as they had, the Civil Rights Act of 1964 would most likely have taken several additional years to pass.

In the North, desegregation moved much more in accordance with the Supreme Courts ruling, but civil rights demonstrations still increased there, some peaceful, others not. The long, hot summers of the mid-1960's would see race riots consume whole sections of most major cities throughout the country. And most whites could not understand the reason for it at a time when it seemed like blacks were winning most of what they were demanding. But Martin Luther King pointed out that, "to the blacks who had been deprived of so much for so long and constantly told to be patient and wait, that wait came to mean never and the Negro could wait no more."

The tumultuous decade of the 1960's began with demonstrations and mob violence and it ended with assassinations. The one man who embodied the peaceful civil rights movement the most—Dr. Martin Luther King Jr.—was shot to death in Memphis, Tennessee, on April 4, 1968. Then before the country could come to grips with that loss, much less recover from it, the great white hope of civil rights—Bobby Kennedy—was gunned down while campaigning for the presidency in Los Angeles. Many people have wondered what might have been had they both lived. It would be hard not to imagine a better America. But in the grand scheme of things, both King and Kennedy had already established their legacy. Their deaths if anything propelled the civil rights movement further and faster. And again history would be so cruel that those who gave so much to a cause would never live to see it reach fruition.

Though remnants of racial discrimination still persist decades later today, they are much more subtle and therefore harder to combat. This situation is now further complicated by reverse discrimination. But discrimination of the magnitude that we have experienced in this country, once set into motion and perpetuated for two-hundred years, will probably continue to plague the U.S. for some time to come.

# XI

---

## The Right to Protest Suspended

*"Those who suppress freedom always do so in the name of law and order."*

*—John V. Lindsay*

The very first amendment to the United States Constitution guarantees the right of the people to peaceably assemble and petition the government for redress of grievances. But there have been many instances when this sacred promise made by the government to the people has been broken. This most frequently tends to happen during times of public discontent over hot political issues or threat of war. Typically, whenever the right to protest has been suspended, authorities will use the volatile public atmosphere as a pretext for squelching political dissent over and above any actual threat to national security. To recount all of these instances would fill volumes, but the following are three of the most dramatic instances.

# CRUSHING THE BONUS ARMY (Washington DC. 1932)

Politicians thrive on and survive on popularity. They live for achieving that vote of confidence of one half of the electorate plus one that wins an election. What a thrill it must be to win an election, especially an election to the highest office in the land—President of the United States. And how frustrating it must be to weld this enormous power but be powerless to stop thousands of protestors demonstrating right on their front doorstep, accusing you of being heartless and uncaring to the people's needs or being a baby killer through the execution of a war.

Yet this masochist ritual is very much part of the job of being the president. Most presidents have endured this burden with restraint and varying degrees of grace. One that did not was our 31st president— Herbert Hoover.

On May 19, 1924, Congress passed legislation, over the veto of then President Coolidge, allocating $2 billion dollars as a bonus to be paid to veterans of the First World War, with payments set to begin in 1945. Then just five years later came the stock market crash and the Great Depression, which brought with it the most desperate economic times the country had ever known.

To the veterans and their families it made no sense to struggle to survive from day to day when they had this sizable asset sitting idle in some bank. Especially when it could provide a great deal of the relief they so desperately needed. So it was with this very simple rationale in mind that thousands of unemployed and destitute veterans marched on Washington to petition for the early payment of their bonus.

President Hoover, however, refused to even consider their request. As a result, the "Bonus Army" as they would come to be known decided to set up camp around the White House and fight a war of attrition with the president.

It was a demonstration that greatly frustrated the president because he could not get away from it or ignore it, since the Bonus Army had surrounded the White House. After several weeks of this annoyance, the president apparently saw no reason to put up with the veterans anymore. He did after all have the entire United States Army at his disposal, which could so easily sweep them from the city and his conscience.

On July 28, 1932, Hoover delivered his ultimatum, ordering the veterans to leave the city or be unceremoniously run out of town. When the veterans made it clear they would not leave at his request, President Hoover ordered federal troops under the command of General Douglas MacArthur to forcibly evict them. Upon issuing the order, the president explained he had the sudden revelation that communists had infiltrated the protesters. Invoking the great communist bogeyman in this manner would of course become a frequent practice in silencing political dissent over the next half century.

Eyewitnesses, including many soldiers who had participated in the rout, described it as a barbaric scene. MacArthur led his present-day troops against his former comrades, with sabers drawn and bayonets fixed. Tanks and tear gas backed up the cavalry. The veterans in many cases were brutally beaten, stabbed, and gassed. It was combat all over again for the veterans of the Great War, only this time they were unarmed and the attacking force was the very government they had risked life and limb to defend just a few short years before.

The cavalry torched the tent and shantytowns the veterans had constructed and the veterans were run out of the capital, just as President Hoover had threatened. MacArthur exclaimed afterwards, "I felt revolution in the air." His more somber aide, Major Dwight D. Eisenhower, however stated, "it was a pitiful scene, that never should have been permitted to happen." The casualties totaled one dead and 65 wounded. Many historians believe that it was Hoover's harsh treatment of the veterans that sealed the fate of his re-election bid and swept Franklin D. Roosevelt and his "New Deal" into the White House four months later.

## Chicago—The Greatest Democratic City on Earth

Nineteen Sixty-eight was a convulsive year in America. The country was torn apart over the long and protracted war in Vietnam and demonstrations against it became daily routines throughout the country. With many blacks becoming more impatient due to 100 years of promises unkept, race riots consumed whole cities across the country during that hot summer. And as if these two volatile movements were not devastating enough, in April and again in June of that year the two most promising leaders of peace and healing in this country—civil rights leader Dr. Martin Luther King Jr. and Senator Robert F. Kennedy—were assassinated. Many of those who lived through those turbulent times wondered if there was anyone or anything left to believe in. The divisiveness of the country would culminate that year at the Democratic National Convention in Chicago.

The Mayor of Chicago, Richard J. Daley, was the last of the big-city bosses. He was from the old school of "might makes right" and you don't question authority. With the approach of the Democratic Convention and the hordes of anti-war protesters about to descend upon his city, Daley knew he was about to confront the most untraditional and politically unorthodox youths ever to assemble. While there would be many Vietnam War veterans and others who would participate in the protests in Chicago, the movement was mostly identified with the hippies—young Americans opposed to the Vietnam War in particular and many of the failures of society in general. They advocated an immediate withdrawal of all American troops from Vietnam, as well as the abdication of America's role as a world super power. It was destined to be the ultimate clash of the generation gap. For his part, Daley was determined to see to it that the "hippies" did not disrupt the Democratic National Convention.

Chicago's preparation for the convention was more like preparation for a war. Barricade fences with barbed wire were erected and heavily armed police were positioned on the rooftops of surrounding building and overpasses. One UPI news correspondent, Richard Longworth, who had just returned from the Soviet Union, noted that it was easier to get into the Kremlin than Chicago's Amphitheater. He also noted that entering the Amphitheater required passing through five separate checkpoints, which were three more than it took to enter East Berlin. Security was so tight, in fact, that police even turned way Speaker of the House John MacCormack, who had all appropriate clearance and identification. The press dubbed this the DMZ—Daley's Militarized Zone.

Further measures included National Guard units being placed on alert. The Guard prepared for crowd control by mounting five-foot-by-four-foot sections of barbed-wire fence onto the fronts of their jeeps. These were designed not merely to clear crowds, but to cut them to ribbons as well. This action would have been deemed cruel if perpetrated against cattle, much less people. After viewing them, the press dubbed these devices "Daley's Dozers."

Just as the rest of the country was sharply divided over the war, the Democratic Party that year was exhibiting schizophrenic characteristics as well, being split between the "Hawks" who were the die hard supporters of the Vietnam War and the "Doves" who were calling for an immediate withdrawal.

On Sunday, August 25, 1968, 7,500 anti-war protestors from all across the country began converging on Chicago. Most could not afford hotel accommodations, even though there were few to be had, so they congregated in Lincoln Park.

While many of these protesters were radical in many of their political beliefs, they were also American citizens intending to do no more than exercise their First Amendment right to petition their government for change. The financial status of the mostly college students not being able to afford the inflated prices of accommodations in a city playing host to a national convention can by no means be considered a reason to void the First Amendment. They had a right to protest the war and the time and place was in fact most appropriate, since this was the political party largely responsible for the execution of the war.

The protesters came to Chicago determined to have their say. And many of them knew full well that there would likely be a price to pay for that say. They knew they were about to confront a hard-nosed mayor who had little patience for civil disobedience and who would be all too willing to use overwhelming force to subdue them and run them out of town. This was, after all, the same Mayor Daley who during the civil disturbances following Martin Luther King Jr.'s assassination had given "shoot to kill" orders to his police. Daley had also made it clear that he was determined to do whatever he had to in order to prevent embarrassment to the city and the Democratic Party.

The protest leaders believed their only hope lay with the presence of the news media. They reasoned that this would either cause the mayor to use some degree of restraint or barring that at least expose his heavy handedness.

Monday was the first night of the convention and the stench of manure from the nearby slaughterhouses hung heavy in the air. As evening fell the police began their well-planned attack against the protesters, who up to this time were loud and obnoxious but peaceful in their protesting. They raised the American flag upside down and chanted "Dump the Hump," referring to the impending nomination of Vice President Hubert Humphrey as the Democrats presidential nominee. The police fired tear gas into the crowds and then proceeded to attack the protesters, beating them savagely with nightsticks.

Prior to the attack and betraying their own conscience, all of the police had removed their badges, nameplates, precinct patches, and anything else that might help to identify them. It quickly became apparent that the police were nothing more than a state-sponsored mob that was out of control. The police had no intention of enforcing the law or preserving the peace. And their attack was not just limited to the protesters, as it was also open season on reporters, bystanders and anyone else unfortunate enough to be anywhere near the vicinity of the protests. In fact, reporters quickly became their targets of choice, especially photographers who had the potential of providing irrefutable evidence of their brutality.

Only after this brutal and unprovoked attack by police did the protesters retaliate by throwing bricks, bottles, and anything else they could lay their hands on. At this point, it truly became a riot, though a riot caused by the police. But as bad as it was, this first night of rioting was just a prelude of things to come.

The next day would be dubbed Bloody Tuesday by the press. This was the day that was said to be the worst of all. Many clergy went to Lincoln Park on Tuesday night to appeal to the protesters to lay down their bricks and bottles and rededicate themselves to a peaceful protest. In a symbolic gesture, the clergymen erected a large wooden cross in the middle of the crowd.

Shortly thereafter, the police surrounded the demonstrators and ordered everyone to vacate the park in 5 minutes. But being surrounded by club-welding police, there was nowhere to go. Exactly five minutes later tear gas canisters were lobbed into the crowd and the police again began their attack, swinging their clubs with a vengeance. The crowd again picked up their bottles and rocks and fought for their lives as the clergymen took down their cross and retreated.

News correspondence reported that they witnessed spectators being attacked by the rabid police in and around the park, as were rescue workers who tried to administer aid to the injured. Senator George McGovern said the brutality of the police made him sick to his stomach and that the scenes were reminiscent of Nazi Germany.

On this night, the violence even spread to inside the convention hall, where police clubbed and beat delegates and newsmen in the frenzy. The always cool and collected CBS news anchor, Walter Cronkite, called the guards "thugs" after his colleague, Dan Rather, was punched in the stomach and ordered to "get the hell out of here," when he tried to cover the disturbance on the convention floor. Senator Abraham Ribicoff took to the podium and accused the Chicago police of using "Gestapo tactics." Mayor Daley responded with a demand to, "Throw the Jew out."

Each night for the next three nights the police would clear the park shortly after the 11:00 p.m. curfew. And each morning the protesters, having no place else to go, would reclaim the park and the chain of events would repeat all over again.

When the protesters were tear gassed out of Lincoln Park on Wednesday night, they reassembled at Grant Park right across the street from the Conrad Hilton Hotel, which was the headquarters of the Democratic National Convention and housed most of the delegates and many reporters.

At 3 a.m., speakers began taking turns calling for an end to the war and protesting their treatment. They then proceeded to sing "This Land Is Your Land" and "We Shall Overcome."

Because of increased media presence, the police were ordered not to attack the protesters there. At this point, National Guardsmen took up positions around the park after replacing the police.

The Guardsmen came with all the weaponry of war. Rifles were ready, bayonets fixed, tanks and trucks rolled into town, and the notorious Daley's Dozers stood ready—all under the guise of preserving the peace and ensuring justice.

During those violent days in August 1968, there seemed little difference between the war in Vietnam and the war in Chicago, except for the terrain. Earlier, when Chicago city officials found out that the protesters were planning to stage a march to the convention center on the last night of the convention, they announced that they were going to require permits for any marches. They then promptly refused to issue any because of public safety concerns.

The protesters announced they were going to march with or without a permit, citing that "they need permits in Russia, this is America." They then called out towards the Conrad Hilton Hotel and asked the delegates there to join them in their march to the convention center the next night. They also asked them to show their support for them by blinking the lights in their rooms off and on. To everyone's amazement, dozens of lights started blinking.

On Thursday night, several delegates did march to Grant Park to join the protesters. As the demonstrators marched from Grant Park to the convention center, the Chicago police and National Guardsmen, acting on Mayor Daley's orders to stop them at all costs, met them.

As the protesters came into sight of the convention center and met up with the phalanx of police, witnesses and newsmen said the police acted like Nazis while screaming, "We'll kill all you bastards." Protesters responded by calling them "pigs" and saying, "the world is watching." And watching the world was. Unlike previous instances where the right to protest was suspended, such as the routing of the Bonus Army from Washington D.C. in 1932, this time the cameras were rolling and the world bore witness. The protesters were beaten with clubs and tear gassed by the police. Ultimately, 700 protesters would be injured and 650 would be arrested.

The environment inside of the convention center mimicked the state of siege outside. While there were only sporadic violent attacks by police against delegates and news correspondents on this night, any semblance of democracy in the Democratic National Convention was dispelled when twenty members of one states' delegation, opposed to the nomination of Hubert Humphrey, were arrested when they refused to listen to his acceptance speech.

One newsman suggested that the iron-fisted despots in the Kremlin must have been pleased and further suggested that Chairman Kosygin might request the loan of Mayor Daley's police in the future.

Mayor Daley won the battle with the overwhelming force of his police and the Illinois National Guard, but in the end, it was freedom of speech that won out in Chicago, though at a terrible price. Thousands of protesters were beaten and bloodied, their bones broken, their lungs gassed, all to exercise a right that the United States Constitution said was already supposed to be theirs. A right that they had been told was bought and paid for on the countless battlefields where American soldiers had fought and died. But, the fact is all of our greatest battles for freedom and democracy have and will continue to be waged within our own borders.

# The Kent State Massacre—May 4, 1970

Before 1970, Kent State University was a quiet campus that most people had never heard of. But since May 4, 1970, Kent State is a name that has become synonymous with deadly force used to silence political dissent. It was unthinkable that such a thing could have happened on a college campus in America, even in light of the violent opposition to the Vietnam War taking place at that time.

The chain of events that led up to the Kent State Massacre began on Thursday night, April 30, 1970. President Nixon addressed the nation and announced that he had ordered troops into Cambodia to attack communist bases of operation from which enemy attacks were being directed across the border into South Vietnam. This expansion of the war immediately ignited increased anti-war demonstrations on college campuses across the country, including Kent State in Ohio.

The anti-war demonstrations on college campuses across the nation were growing progressively more violent. The ROTC building on the Kent State campus was set afire by arsonists the previous week. It was in this setting that Ohio Governor James Rhodes ordered the National Guard in to break up "all" anti-war demonstrations, after citing the familiar and by now predictable accusation that it was his belief that the anti-war student protests were "communist inspired."

The National Guard troops, numbering about 100, moved in on about 600 protesters and ordered them to disperse. The students refused, at which time the troops moved in with bayonets and tear gas. The students responded by throwing rocks. The guardsmen began retreating, and then without warning opened fire into the crowd of unarmed students. The result was four students killed and ten wounded. It was a scene reminiscent of the Boston Massacre of 1770 when British troops fired on and killed four colonists protesting the King's oppression.

Most states do not issue live ammunition to National Guardsman detailed to riot control, opting instead for the more non-lethal weapons such as tear gas and nightsticks. But in Ohio, National Guard units this time moved out prepared for war. The Guard commander stated after the fact that his troops thought they heard a gun shot prior to firing into the crowd. But no weapons were ever found at the scene and the fact that the National Guard fired randomly into such a large crowd left little chance that the troops would have found their mark even if a legitimate target did exist.

Ironically, student leaders maintained that none of those killed were even participating in the rally. In fact, one dead student was identified as a 19-year-old ROTC cadet. Another student was 19-year-old Allison Krause, who was killed along with her boyfriend, when they stopped to see what was going on. She had just gotten off the phone with her parents, and in her final conversation with them, expressed resentment towards the anti-war protesters. However, in the aftermath of her death, her shocked father asked, "Is dissent a crime?" Many newspapers eulogized the students as the home front casualties of the Vietnam War. President Nixon, upon hearing of the incident, said only that, "…it should convince educators and students alike that when dissent turns to violence, it invites tragedy."

In October, a presidential commission appointed to investigate the incident warned the president that, "…he must solve this political crises that has no parallel in the history of our nation."

The Vietnam War would continue to bleed the United States of financial resources, young lives, and morale for three more years. A truce was finally signed on January 27, 1973, officially ending hostilities between all the combatants, and the United States finally withdrew.

But North Vietnam was well aware that the American public would never permit U.S. troops to return—no matter what. Any remaining doubts they may have had concerning violating the truce evaporated when President Nixon became besieged by threat of impeachment over

Watergate and was rendered powerless by the resultant lack of confidence and support. Shortly thereafter, North Vietnam invaded South Vietnam. And on April 7, 1975, after the sacrifice of over 58,000 American lives, the longest war in American history ended with the fall of Saigon.

# XII

---

## Georgia's Bedroom Police

*"The Founders enacted the Bill of Rights to establish a zone of personal sovereignty into which the government could not intrude, so that the United States would be a place where it is safe to be different."*

*—Ira Glasser, Executive Director, ACLU*

There is probably no right guaranteed by the Bill of Rights that is more basic or sacred than the right to privacy. Although the word "privacy" itself does not actually appear anywhere in the Constitution, its implication is made clear in the Fourth Amendment's pronouncement of: "The right of the people to be secure in their persons, houses, papers, and effects..."

Few people would argue that at the core of the right to privacy would be those most intimate affairs of people; namely the sexual relationships between consenting adults when conducted within the privacy of their bedroom. So it was the epitome of violating the spirit and intent of the Fourth Amendment's freedom of privacy when Michael Hardwick was arrested for engaging in a sex act that was forbidden by the state of Georgia. His accomplice was another consenting adult and the scene of the crime was his own bedroom.

The law in question was Georgia's sodomy law. That law states that an act of sodomy has occurred anytime "a person performs or submits to any sex act involving the sex organ of one person, with either the mouth or anus of another..." Violation of this law carries a prison sentence of 20 years. Amazingly, this arrest did not take place during the puritanical days of the 1680's but rather during the 1980's.

In 1982, a police officer went to Michael Hardwick's house to serve a warrant for an overdue fine. The housekeeper let him in. The officer then began walking through the house and eventually came to Hardwick's bedroom where he witnessed Hardwick performing oral sex on another man. The officer arrested Hardwick and charged him with violating Georgia's sodomy law.

The Fulton County District Attorney, Lewis Slaton, probably sensed the absurdity of the situation and declined to prosecute the case, "unless further evidence came to light." But Hardwick felt that such a ridiculous and outdated law surely had to be unconstitutional and that it should be struck from the books. So he filed suit in Federal District Court seeking an injunction against the law.

The Federal District Court refused to rule on the constitutionality of the law in question and dismissed the suit on the grounds that Hardwick was no longer being prosecuted for the crime. But Hardwick was not satisfied to have the court ignore the true problem at hand; permitting a law to remain in effect for no other obvious reason than selective enforcement. So he appealed the dismissal of the suit to the District Court of Appeals.

A divided panel on the Court of Appeals ruled that the Georgia law did violate Hardwick's fundamental rights, stating, "...his sexual activity is a private and intimate association that is beyond the reach of the state's regulation by reason of the Ninth Amendment, (which states that the rights of the individual are not limited to just those specifically listed in the Constitution) and the Due Process Clause of the Fourteenth Amendment." Because other Courts of Appeals had arrived at judgments contrary to this ruling, the Attorney General requested that the United States Supreme Court review the case.

On March 31, 1986, the United States Supreme Court agreed to review the case. On June 30$^{th}$, they made the incredible ruling by a five-to-four decision, against Hardwick's claim of right to privacy and upholding the constitutionality of Georgia's sodomy law.

Justice White delivered the Court's opinion and was joined by Justices Burger, Powell, Renquist, and O'Connor. "We first register our disagreement with the Court of Appeals and with the respondent (Mr. Hardwick) that the Court's prior cases have construed the Constitution to confer a right of privacy that extends to homosexual sodomy that for all intents and purposes have decided this case. No connection between family, marriage, or procreation on the one hand and homosexual activity on the other has been demonstrated either by the Court of Appeals or by the respondent (Mr. Hardwick)."

"Sodomy was a criminal offense at common law and was forbidden by the laws of all of the 13 original states when they ratified the Bill of Rights. In fact, until 1961, all 50 States outlawed sodomy and today 24 States and the District of Columbia continue to provide criminal penalties for sodomy even if performed in private and between consenting adults. There should be, therefore, great resistance to expand the substantive reach of those clauses, particularly if it requires redefining the category of rights deemed to be fundamental."

Justice White further wrote that, "The respondent (Mr. Hardwick) asserts that even if the conduct here is not a fundamental right, there must be a rational basis for the law and that there is none in this case other than the presumed belief of a majority of the electorate in Georgia that homosexual sodomy is immoral and unacceptable".

"The law is, however, constantly based on notions of morality and if all laws representing essentially moral choices are to be invalidated under the Due Process Clause, the courts will be very busy indeed."

Justice Burger added to the Courts opinion that, "Condemnation of those (homosexual) practices is firmly rooted in Judeo-Christian moral and ethical standards. Homosexuality was a capital crime under Roman law. Blackstone described the infamous crime against nature as an offense of deeper malignity than rape…a heinous act."

"This is not a question of personal preferences but rather of the legislative authority of the state. I find nothing in the Constitution depriving a state of the power to enact the statute challenged here."

Justice Powell also concurred but added that, "Mr. Hardwick may be protected by the 8th amendment (forbidding cruel and unusual punishment) with regards to imprisonment of up to 20 years, but was not prosecuted."

And so, it was that with this ruling America's new conservative Supreme Court struck the most obnoxious blow to the constitutional right to privacy in the history of the United States. Their ruling went well beyond respectable conservatism and plunged deeply into totalitarianism by attempting to put conformity above respect for the right of the people to form intimate associations of their own preference. Until this ruling, the sexual relations of adult citizens were an area that was generally accepted to be beyond the reach of the government. But by the force of their ruling, the United States Supreme Court said that the government has the right to prosecute its citizens for engaging in certain types of consensual sex acts even if taking place in the privacy of their own bedroom.

This case as brought before the Supreme Court was no more about a fundamental right to engage in "homosexual sodomy," as the court cited, than previous rulings that overturned convictions of people accused of reading material considered by some to be pornographic was about a fundamental right to read pornographic books. It is rather a question of whether a person has the right to read what they choose to read, think what they choose to think, and live their lives the way they chose to live without government interference. Because if the right to privacy means anything at all, it must mean that people have the right to be left alone with regards to their most intimate relationships.

President Reagan, whose appointments made this new conservative court possible, promised during the campaign of 1980 that if elected he would get the government off the backs of the people. What he failed to tell us was his intention to invade our bedrooms.

The Court asserted in its ruling that the right to privacy exists strictly for purposes of marriage, procreation, child rearing, and abortion. But here the court not only gives the narrowest of interpretations of the United States Constitution, they also turn a blind eye to the promise of all citizens having the "unalienable rights...[of] life, liberty, and the pursuit of happiness" as mentioned in the Declaration of Independence.

Justice Blackmun observed in his dissenting opinion that, "We protect those rights (to privacy) not because they contribute in some direct and material way to the general public welfare, but because they form so central a part of an individual's life. The concept of privacy embodies the moral fact that a person belongs to himself and not others nor to society as a whole."

Georgia's sodomy law generically states that any act where the sex organ of one person comes into contact with either the mouth or anus of another person is in violation of this law and holds the participants subject to a 20-year prison sentence. This law gives no mention to where the act takes place, who the participants may be, or any other circumstances. So a married, heterosexual couple engaging in a similar act would be just as liable under the provisions of this law. Given this fact, even the most conservative homophobes would probably choose to invalidate this law. But the Supreme Court did not consider determining the constitutionality of the law itself. The Court was rather totally obsessed by the participants being homosexual in this particular case. It persistently qualified all of its references to "sodomy" as "homosexual sodomy," thus substantiating Georgia's policy of enforcing against homosexuals a law it has no apparent desire to enforce against heterosexuals, even though the acts are identical. This is selective enforcement and as such is clearly prejudicial and offensive to the whole concept of full and equal protection under the law.

Georgia's sodomy law, as all such laws that remain on the books today, was written centuries ago in total ignorance of any clear understanding of human sexuality. Today you would be hard pressed to find any psychologist, psychiatrist or sociologist that would tell you that oral sex is abnormal, amoral or in any way unhealthy.

The normalcy of this act has in fact been verified by every major scientific study conducted on the subject of human sexuality over the last half century. They include the research of such respected and well-known authorities as Masters and Johnson, Alfred Kinsey and Shere Hite (*The Hite Report*). All of these studies have indicated that at this point in time more people engage in oral sex than do not. This hardly qualifies such practices as deviant by definition, nor does it lend any justification for keeping such outdated and largely unenforceable laws on the books.

But in their decision, the Court chose to reminisce back to the days of 1776 when sodomy was illegal in all thirteen states. They then observed that it still remains illegal in some 24 states today, ignoring the fact that repealing these antiquated laws is clearly the direction in which the country as a whole is headed.

Justice Blackmun attacked the Court's nostalgic approach by stating, "I believe that it is revolting to have no better reason for a rule of law than that so it was laid down in the time of (King) Henry IV. It is still more revolting if the grounds upon which it was laid down have vanished long since and the rule simply persists from blind imitation of the past.

"This case…cannot justify invading the houses, hearts, and minds of citizens who choose to live their lives differently. I can only hope that the Court will soon reconsider its analysis and conclude that depriving individuals of the right to choose for themselves how to conduct their intimate relationships poses a far greater threat to the values most deeply rooted in our nation's history than tolerance of non-conformity could ever do. Because I think the Court today betrays those values, I dissent.

"The court also put forth in their majority opinion that sodomy is a practice condemned by the Judeo-Christian religions. Here the court continues to falter in their duty to interpret the law based on the United States Constitution and instead opts to advance religious doctrines. Apparently forgetting the concept of separation of church and state, as well as the fact that they were appointed to be Justices of the Supreme Court of the United States and not Justices of the Supreme Court of Christianity or any other particular religion.

"And finally, even if the Justices voting in the majority did not believe that a homosexual citizen of the United States has a right to participate in a particular sex act with another consenting adult while in the privacy of his own home, but did feel that the law was unconstitutional for any other reason, they should have voted to declared it so. Instead, as if to add insult to injury, in the same written opinion that upheld the Georgia law, Justice Powell closes with the caveat, that the law may be unconstitutional because its 20-year prison sentence may violate the Eighth Amendments guarantee against cruel or unusual punishment.

"But in their willful blindness the Court forgot the question before them. The whole reason for the Supreme Court reviewing this case was not to strike down Michael Hardwick's sentence, because the District Attorney declined to prosecute him. Rather the question before the Court was, is Georgia's sodomy law constitutional in late-twentieth-century America? And if it is not for any reason then the court is morally obligated to invalidate it.

"It is ludicrous for such a ruling to be dependent upon the victim of a bad law putting forward in his complaint the exact mechanism by which the offending law should be struck down. This is the duty of the

Supreme Court Justice, as the typical citizen knows no more about what makes a law constitutional than a rickshaw driver would know what makes the space shuttle fly."

The *Hardwick vs. Bowers* case is a perfect example of how fragile our hold is on even the most basic civil liberties. It shows how vulnerable our rights are and how they can be snatched away from us so much quicker than the time it took to win them. And, ironically how most often these threats are perpetrated by the very people we trust most to "protect and defend the Constitution of the United States" so help them God. This case also quite dramatically marked the end of a half-century of advances in civil liberties, a period of time where the United States Supreme was the champion of civil liberties. It was also the most poignant case to reflect the swing to the far right of the United States Supreme Court, following six years of conservative rule in the White House.

But that swing to the right did not end there. In addition to President Reagan's two appointments to the Court and elevation of the most conservative Justice, William Renquist, to Chief Justice, Reagan's Vice President and immediate successor, George Bush, made two more appointments. In the end, Presidents Reagan and Bush left America with a conservative court that will continue to hold great influence over of the lives of Americans for decades beyond their own terms of office. Consequently, the prognosis for civil liberties has not looked so bleak since the days immediately preceding the Civil War.

The very week after the Hardwick decision was issued, on July 4, 1986, an Independence Day extravaganza was held in New York Harbor to commemorate the 100th anniversary of the Statue of Liberty. It was billed as "Liberty Weekend." The Battleship U.S.S. Iowa played host to President Reagan, as he observed an international naval review. The festivity also included a glitzy all-star cast of Hollywood entertainers and was topped off by a spectacular fireworks display. But this particular

Fourth of July celebration rang somewhat hollow given the Supreme Court decision of the previous week.

# XIII

---

## The Greatest Case of Voter Fraud in History

*"You must at all times insist upon your rights, and here I am not only referring to those rights already accorded you, but others still denied."*

*—Senator Charles Sumner*

Every American school child is taught that we in the United States, unlike most people of the world, enjoy the inalienable right of electing our president. Permitting the people to go through all the motions of a Democratic election only to have their vote ignored and replaced in the end by the only vote that really matters—the Electoral College vote—then further perpetuates this charade. Fortunately, in most elections, the people and the Electoral College have chosen the same person as president, even though there is almost always a great disparity between those two votes.

The Electoral College has been around as long as the presidency itself. At the Constitutional Convention of 1787, there was a great deal of debate over how the president should be elected. While many suggestions were made, they eventually coalesced into two basic schools of thought. All of those considered to be the true geniuses of their day, such as Thomas Jefferson and Benjamin Franklin, were true believers in the ultimate wisdom of the people and advocated the direct popular election of the president. The opposition was lead by John Adams, who argued that the common man was not capable of making an intelligent decision of such importance and favored the state legislatures electing the president.

After much debate, the great compromise was struck; whereby a new institution was created called the Electoral College. Each state would be allotted a number of votes in the Electoral College equal to the sum of their representation in Congress (i.e. total number of U.S. Senators and Representatives). This compromise was overwhelmingly, though not unanimously, adopted. Pennsylvania was the only state to vote against it and all other alternatives to the direct democratic election of the president.

And so it was that the United States Constitution reserved the absolute authority of electing the president not to the people but rather the Electoral College, which for all intents and purposes is nothing more than a band of nameless, faceless, unaccountable politicians. So insignificant in fact is the popular or people's vote, that nowhere in the United States Constitution is it even so much as mentioned.

Most people are aware that the Electoral College exists, but very few understand how it really works. The author of this book contacted the offices of two U.S. Senators, two congressmen, two state senators, and two state representatives from his home state of Pennsylvania, as well as the State Board of Elections and the Federal Election Commission. They were all asked a very simple question: How are the Electors of the Electoral College chosen? There were countless transferred calls and even a few returned calls the next day. But, remarkably, not a single one of these offices were able to answer the question.

The fact that the system responsible for electing the highest and single most powerful official in our country is so obscure and secretive that so few people understand how it works is a red flag in itself. If the process is not corrupt, it is certainly corruptible, as we will soon see.

Article II, Section 1 of the United States Constitution states simply that, "the Electors of the several states shall elect the president." It goes on to say that the states may choose their electors anyway they see fit. The news media reports that most states today choose their electors at their state's Democratic and Republican Party conventions held just prior to the national conventions. But the people never find out who these electors are, or what their unique qualifications are to elect a president on their behalf. And contrary to popular belief there is no constitutional obligation for these electors, once selected to give any consideration whatsoever to the popular vote when casting their ballot.

Traditionally, the Electoral College vote is a state-by-state, winner-take-all contest, which only further serves to distort the popular vote and increases the likelihood that the loser of the popular vote could still be installed as president.

For example, California currently has 54 votes or one-fifth of all the Electoral votes needed to win the election. If Presidential Candidate Number One were to win California by just one popular (real person) vote, under this winner-take-all tradition, he or she would walk away with all of California's 54 Electoral votes. Candidate Number Two, who in a close election might capture 49.9% of the vote, would get nothing. Those 49.9% of Californians who voted for Candidate Number Two would in effect be disenfranchised, losing their election voice completely. Candidate Number Two could then go on to win by huge margins of votes in several smaller states, taking all of their corresponding but numerically less significant Electoral votes and possibly winning the popular vote nationwide by a significant margin, but still lose the Electoral vote and therefore the election.

The above scenario is if the Electoral College votes according to tradition. But as previously stated, the electors once chosen are under no obligation to do anything except cast their vote. There has in fact already been several times when electors have not cast their vote the way they were traditionally supposed to. In those cases where electors decided to cast their vote as their own personal vote and contrary to the people's wishes they are supposed to be representing, it has always been upheld as valid and final, with no constitutional or legal recourse. Additionally, no punitive action has ever been taken against any "renegade elector" and for good reason. The electors and their votes are left untouchable, with the full protection of the highest law of the land— the United States Constitution.

We are fortunate that the Electoral College has not as of yet used their unique power to initiate their own political coup. But unbeknownst to most people, we may have already come dangerously close to just such a scenario. In 1960, the electors of several Southern states that were opposed to the liberalism of John F. Kennedy supposedly held a clandestine meeting to consider casting their votes for vice presidential candidate Lyndon Johnson instead. After much debate, it was decided against doing so and a constitutional crisis was averted. But only because they did not have enough votes to pull it off. If they had decided to ignore the will of the people, their decision—not the peoples—would have prevailed and there would have been nothing anyone could have done about it until 1964.

This lack of any true democratic process in our presidential election is not just a problem in theory. Four times now, the worst nightmare for a democratic people have come to pass when the people's election of a president was vetoed by the Electoral College system.

In 1824, the people elected Andrew Jackson to the presidency, but when he fell short of winning a majority of electoral votes, the election was thrown into the House of Representatives where John Quincy Adams was named the sixth president of the United States. In 1876, Samuel Tilden convincingly won the popular vote, but the Electoral College thought better of it and elected Rutherford B. Hayes as the nineteenth president of the United States. In 1888, Grover Cleveland won the popular vote but lost the election when the Electoral College installed Benjamin Harrison as our twenty-third president. And, of course, there was Election 2000, where one state held the rest of the country hostage for 36 days until the United States Supreme Court finally intervened to install a president against the will of the majority of the American people.

Those who support the current Electoral College system typically include only the most hard-core party politicians or those who may have benefited by it the last time around. Their best argument is that since the electoral vote is state oriented as opposed to people oriented, it compels the presidential candidates to campaign in all of the states. But this argument holds no water. Since the Electoral College is based on percentage of the population, fifty-one percent of 538 electors or fifty-one percent of 450 million people those electors are supposed to represent is still fifty-one percent. The only difference is the scale of the two votes and the fact that it is much easier to wheel and deal for the votes of 270 electors (i.e. politicians) than 225 million people. Presidential campaign strategies have also always targeted certain states over other states based on the strengths and weaknesses of their candidate.

This was, in fact, how Rutherford B. Hayes stole the election in 1876. Late on election night, after it was already apparent that Samuel Tilden had won the popular vote, Hayes and his lieutenants worked the electors through the night. When the sun came up the next morning, Rutherford B. Hayes was the president-elect and Samuel Tilden was relegated to a footnote in history.

Electoral College advocates also argue for retaining the Electoral College because it lessens the chance of factionalism. In other words, if a strong, third-party candidate could capture enough votes to deprive either of the two major party candidates of a majority (50 percent plus 1) of the vote, he or she would then be in a position to extort concessions from one of the other two candidates in exchange for their support. But this exact scenario has already happened under the current Electoral College system.

In the election of 1824, the vote was split between several candidates, with the top three being Andrew Jackson—41 percent, John Quincy Adams—30 percent and Henry Clay—12 percent. Because no one received a majority of electoral votes, the election was thrown into the House of Representatives. Predictably, all factors were carefully considered except the will of the people. In this particular case, John Quincy Adams was ultimately elected president when Henry Clay threw his support behind him in return for a promise to be appointed Secretary of State. This came to be known as the "corrupt deal," the publicizing of which effectively doomed any hope of re-election for John Quincy Adams. It also resulted in the people being governed for four years by a man they clearly did not want as their president.

Many attempts have been made in Congress over the years to abolish the Electoral College and replace it with a direct democratic election, which the American people would overwhelmingly opt for if given the choice. But Congress is not made up of people, it is made of politicians who collectively seem determined to keep the real power of electing the highest and most powerful office in this country safely out of the hands of the people.

Of all the attempts to abolish the Electoral College, we probably came closest to succeeding in 1969, after a close, three-way race between Richard Nixon, Hubert Humphrey, and George Wallace. Richard Nixon won that close election after losing another close one in 1960. Shortly after being inaugurated, he publicly endorsed presidential election reform. The subsequent resolution that was introduced in Congress called for replacing the Electoral College with a direct popular election. If no candidate were to capture at least 40 percent of the vote, a run-off election between the two candidates winning the most votes would be held within 30 days.

Not only would this system have given the people the vote up front, it would also have given them the final say in a run-off if necessary, as opposed to having to hand the election over to the House of

Representatives, as is currently the case. Under this proposed system, only one election to date would have necessitated a run-off, as opposed to two elections having already been determined by the House of Representatives.

The House of Representatives overwhelmingly passed the Nixon-endorsed resolution. Unfortunately, the United States Senate was determined to see to it that this power not be taken away from the states' Democratic and Republican parties, even in the name of democracy. They filibustered, and the resolution died without ever being voted on.

President Nixon, always the consummate politician, who on so many other occasions would aggressively lobby Congress and, if necessary, go over their heads to the American people to push legislation, failed to effectively bring the full prestige of the presidency to bare on this issue. He took the unique step of publicly endorsing it and then just left it up to Congress to do the right thing. Just as fatal to the resolution's passage was the fact that the press gave scant publicity to an issue that, if passed, would have been the most significant piece of legislation of the twentieth century. As a result, a historic opportunity was lost.

The path to further democratizing our electoral process in this country is not un-blazed. Until 1913, not only were the American people not trusted to elect their president, they were also not trusted to elect their United States Senators. Until the Seventeenth Amendment to the United States Constitution was passed, that right belonged to the state legislatures. One major reason that the Seventeenth Amendment did succeed was probably because the press not only reported the issue but also actively endorsed it. In fact, many historians credit the Hearst newspaper chain with forcing its passage by keeping the spotlight on the issue and the heat on Congress. A vote against democracy would have been very difficult to explain to constituents back home. But newspapers today no longer actively participate in political reform, even when democratic elections are being denied the American people.

For anyone who may have argued that all of these preceding cases were ancient history and said it wouldn't happen again, we now have Election 2000.

It was an unquestionably close election that saw every public opinion poll taken prior to Election Day flip-flopping back and forth. Then finally came the only opinion poll that truly matters, November 7— Election Day. The vote teetered back and forth between Al Gore and George W. Bush for the first hour. Then shortly after eight o'clock, Eastern Standard Time, all the major news networks called the pivotal state of Florida for Al Gore. No sooner had those calls been made than Jeb Bush, the governor of Florida and brother of Republican presidential candidate George W. Bush, called to contest those results. Other numbers came out of Florida shortly afterwards and by a matter of just some hundreds of votes. The governor's brother now appeared to have miraculously won the state.

As if this did not make the Florida election look suspicious enough, there were reports of all sorts of "irregularities" being reported out of Florida all day long. The confusing butterfly ballot from Palm Beach County is probably the most well known, but there were other more significant signs of a tainted election. Registered voters being purged from voting rolls, police barricades set up around polling places and not enough ballots available at other polls, and all of these irregularities taking place exclusively in Democratic precincts. Not a single problem was reported in any Republican precinct.

Because the final vote was less than one half of one percent, Florida law required an automatic recount. The recount itself then became the focus of attention. A flurry of lawsuits would be filed as to how and what should be recounted. Gore's attorneys, of course, wanted time-consuming hand counts; while Bush's attorneys stalled for time and tried everything they could to stop all recounting. The battle of recount versus stopping the recount came to a head at the Miami-Dade County Court House on November 22. This was the county where Al Gore stood to gain the most votes, possibly enough to turn the election. It was a surreal scene more reminiscent of Nazi Germany than America. A mob of Bush operatives flown in from all over the country forced their way into the courthouse and physically attacked the vote counters causing the recount to immediately be halted.

Election 2000 would be suspended in limbo for a full 36 days after the voting. And in the end, it would not be the people, but rather the Supreme Court that would determine who the next president would be. On December 12, 2000, the United States Supreme Court issued one of the most controversial decisions in history. By a five-to-four ruling, the Court ordered all recounts to stop immediately, in effect awarding the election to George W. Bush.

In his dissenting opinion, Justice John Paul Stevens stated, "Time will one day heal the wound that will be inflicted by today's decision. One thing, however, is certain. Although we may never know with complete certainty the identity of the winner of this year's presidential election, the identity of the loser is perfectly clear. It is the nation's confidence in the judge as an impartial guardian of the rule of law."

In the final analysis, if America's presidential election was the democratic process it was always portrayed to be, Election 2000 would have been over election night, Florida and her few hundred controversial votes would not have mattered and the winner not the loser of the election would have become president.

# XIV

---

## The Republican Coup d' etat of 1998

*Of all tyrannies, a tyranny exercised for the good of its victims may be the most oppressive....those who torment us for our own good will torment us without end, for they do so with the approval of their consciences.*

—C.S. Lewis

Bill Clinton was the arch nemesis of conservatives for the better part of the 1990's. Slick Willie was the draft dodging, gay loving, skirt chasing, pot smoker that didn't inhale who stepped up to the plate to challenge the Republican's conservative, standard bearer and winner of the Gulf War, George Herbert Walker Bush.

Bill Clinton defeated George Bush in one of the greatest political upsets of the century. And conservatives were left beside themselves with contempt. Prior to this time, there was some civility and acceptance of "the will of the people" after an election, grudgingly though it might have been, but not in 1992. In a very real sense, the next campaign began the day after the last one ended. Some conservatives would take the extraordinary step of publicly stating that, "Bill Clinton is not my president." And in one case, United States Senator Jesse Helms warned the president that he was not welcome in his state, but if he came, he better bring his bodyguards.

It was in this poisonous political atmosphere that conservatives started planning the overthrow of a democratically elected president by extra-political means. But as determined as they were and no one could fault them for not being determined, William Jefferson Clinton would prove to be their worse nightmare of an opponent.

In January 1994, after months of lobbying by congressional Republicans, U.S. Attorney General Janet Reno agreed to appoint an independent counsel to investigate a failed real estate deal that Bill and Hillary Clinton were partners in back in the 1970's known as Whitewater. Unlike the Republicans appointing a member of their own party to investigate the Reagan-Bush, Iran-Contra affair, Reno looked for a respected member of the opposition party. She chose Robert Fiske, a New York lawyer, former U.S. Attorney and a Republican.

James and Susan McDougal formed the Whitewater Development Corporation in 1978. Whitewater was the name given to a real estate project to develop 220 acres of land along the White River in northern Arkansas. In addition to his real estate speculation, James McDougal would, in 1982, years after the Whitewater project, buy the Madison Savings and Loan. It was at this same time that Congress decided to deregulate savings and loans. This deregulation resulted in numerous savings and loans failing, then being bailed out by the United States government. James McDougal joined such other notables as Congressman Fernand St. Germain, Senator Jake Garn, and presidential son, Neil Bush, as beneficiaries of the American taxpayers.

For the Clintons' part in Whitewater, there should not have been much to investigate, since they did not profit, but instead lost $40,000 in the project. But Whitewater was the vehicle by which the political enemies of the president would investigate and harass him for seven of his eight years in office and then some.

The lack of anything resembling credible evidence of wrongdoing on the part of the Clintons should have been relatively quick to determine. But as soon as one investigation would prove baseless, the Office of Independent Counsel would simply expand their investigation into other totally unrelated areas. During his six months as independent counsel, Fiske would end up expanding his real estate investigation of Clinton to also include the firing of five White House travel office employees, the mishandling of FBI files by the White House Security staff and such other ridiculous accusations as whether or not the president of the United States and First Lady murdered White House Counsel Vince Foster.

If Fiske was aggressive and thorough, he might also have been fair. Having found no evidence of criminal wrongdoing by the president, word was getting around that Fiske was preparing to wind down the investigations. Congressional Republicans in 1992, however, were not interested in fairness. Conservative stalwarts Jesse Helms and Lauch Faircloth proceeded to lobby a friendly, three-Republican-judge panel to replace Fiske with their own handpicked man, Kenneth Starr. Their reason for replacing Fiske was conflict of interest, because an attorney general, who was in turn appointed by the president, appointed Fiske.

The conflict of interest of Ken Starr being the solicitor general to President Bush who was the just-defeated opponent of the current president was conveniently ignored. As was the fact that Starr was a lawyer for the tobacco industry and reportedly still receiving payments from them through his old law firm while investigating a president who was actively battling that industry.

Once installed as independent counsel, Starr decided to start all over and build his investigation against Clinton around David Hale, an Arkansas businessman of questionable reliability. Hale would eventually claim that Governor Clinton pressured him to make an illegal loan to James McDougal for the Whitewater project. Starr would use Hale's testimony verbatim, despite the fact that previous investigations had already uncovered that Hale had a long history of falsely invoking Clinton's name, including one scam which involved $50,000 worth of kickbacks from a healthcare company that was seeking an Arkansas contract.

Caryn Mann, Hale's live-in girlfriend, and her teenage son have testified that while cooperating with Starr between 1994 and 1996, Hale stayed rent free at a Hot Spring's resort owned by anti-Clinton activist Parker Dozhier. They also both testified that cash payments were made to Hale from conservative activists Stephen Bonton and David Henderson. Boynton and Henderson were reportedly two of the key overseers of what has come to be known as the "Arkansas Project."

The Arkansas Project was an affiliation of conservative lawyers and businessmen whose personal hatred of Bill Clinton went far beyond normal politics. The Arkansas Project was committed to digging up or manufacturing any disparaging stories they could to embarrass the president. Right-wing activist and billionaire, Richard Mellon Scaife, generously funded the project. Other notable Clinton-haters contributed millions of additional dollars, such as: the National Rifle Association, Phillip Morris, R.J. Reynolds, and other tobacco companies.

The Arkansas Project had at least one direct link to the Office of Independent Counsel. Starr's deputy in Arkansas, Hickman Ewing, met repeatedly with Rex Armistead, the head private detective for the Arkansas Project. Armistead was a less-than-reputable investigator who had previously charged Governor Clinton with being an accomplice to a cocaine smuggling ring operating out of the Mena Airport in Arkansas. This charge, besides being bizarre on its face value considering the fact that the president had his own brother arrested for possession of cocaine, was investigated and rejected by three separate federal judges.

One Whitewater investigator has subsequently expressed concern publicly about Ewing's meeting with Armistead based not only on their appearance, but also because many of their meetings went unrecorded in the meeting logs of the Office of Independent Counsel.

Fueled by their pathological hatred of Bill Clinton and financed by big tobacco, several anti-Clinton groups sprang up whose sole purpose was to destroy the president, politically and personally. One of the more notable groups dubbed themselves "The Elves." The Elves were an organized network of the conservative Republican lawyers in Arkansas, Washington D.C., and New York. They worked extensively and in concert to file nuisance lawsuits and leak salacious material—some true, some false—to sympathetic members of the press. Some of the more well known "Elves" have since been identified as Joe DiGenova, Ted and Barbara Olson, Gil Davis, Joe Cammarata and former Supreme Court nominee, Robert Bork.

But, while the "Arkansas Project" and "the Elves" were practicing black politics with private funding, Kenneth Starr was perpetrating a partisan political vendetta against a democratically elected president using all of the resources of the federal government and fully funded by taxpayer dollars. There was no time or financial limits imposed upon Starr and no oversight—dangerous powers in the wrong hands. And Starr would play fast and loose with his unlimited prosecutorial power. He would end up interrogating some 320 witnesses. Intimidation, coercion, and, in a some cases, jailing uncooperative witnesses in solitary confinement for months on end were just some of the techniques used by the Office of Independent Counsel to get the president.

Starr's office would repeatedly leak secret grand jury testimony to the press. Other confidential information that could embarrass the president was also leaked to a degree not seen since J. Edgar Hoover's pursuit of Martin Luther King Jr., which has since been so roundly condemned. The Starr investigators also went well beyond just taking testimony; they threatened and coerced witnesses to give testimony they wanted to hear, as Monica Lewinsky and others have claimed.

William Watt, a municipal judge from Arkansas, was one person interrogated by Starr's investigators. Watt has since stated to news people that he felt unquestionable pressure by Starr's investigators to give testimony to implicate the president and had leading statements fed to him. Watt also stated that when he disputed their interpretation of his testimony, "they said they didn't like the truth the way I told it…they liked their truth better." Any exculpatory statements Watt made were never documented.

After going to great lengths to publicly expose all of Bill Clinton's personal indiscretions but watching him coast to an easy re-election victory in 1996 against another solid conservative in Bob Dole, leaders of the Christian Coalition and conservative Republicans turned rabid. The leadership of the Republican Party, now in control of both houses of Congress for the first time in 40 years, decided shortly after the election that they would do whatever it took to undo this travesty of democracy and save the American people from themselves.

Despite his best efforts, by spring of 1997, Starr's investigations into Whitewater, Travel-gate, File-gate and the death of Vince Foster had been played for all they could. Public sentiment was quickly building to end what had already become the longest and most expensive political investigation in history. Starr was considering leaving the Office of Independent Counsel to take a job as dean of Pepperdine University.

But then, just as the pursuit of the president looked like it was about to end, the United States Supreme Court handed down a fateful ruling. On May 27, 1997, the Court ruled against the longstanding precedent of presidential immunity from civil suit while in office. This ruling cleared the way for a sexual harassment suit filed by Paula Jones to go forward. In ruling for Paula Jones, the high court rejected the argument that a civil suit against a sitting president would be disruptive to the president or the country. The Court would be proved woefully wrong.

The Paula Jones' lawsuit was based on her claim that, while governor of Arkansas, Bill Clinton propositioned her at The Excelsior Hotel in

Little Rock. The suit has been widely criticized by legal experts as being frivolous due to the fact that Ms. Jones never suffered any damage from the alleged advance. The only reason the suit continued was because it was fully funded by the political enemies of the president and legally aided by "The Elves" solely for the purpose of harassing the president. If it were not for the political motives involved, it is unlikely any lawyer in the country would have filed it.

On January 12, 1998, Kenneth Starr received a phone call from a current White House staffer who was a left over from the Bush administration named Linda Tripp. In the fall of 1997, Ms. Tripp began secretly tape-recording her telephone conversations with a young White House intern named Monica Lewinsky. Under the guise of being a sympathetic friend, Ms. Tripp encouraged Lewinsky to talk extensively about her affair with the president.

Secretly recording telephone conversations of course is illegal and would be inadmissible in any court in the land, but this was just one more trivial detail that did not bother or deter the independent counsel in his boundless pursuit of the president. Ms. Tripp handed over to Starr some 22 hours of illegally recorded telephone conversations between herself and Monica Lewinsky.

With an abundance of new salacious material, Kenneth Starr decided to expand his investigation yet again, this time going for the Achilles Heel of the president. The Office of Independent Counsel assigned with investigating a real estate deal from the 1970's was now going to investigate whether or not the President of the United States received oral sex in the White House. Starr's request to begin investigating the president's sex life was quickly rubber stamped by the same Republican, 3-judge panel that appointed him as independent counsel.

It was at this point that another great conflict of interest came into being that would have disqualified Kenneth Starr from any further involvement in any legitimate court case in America. Just 3 months prior to being appointed independent counsel, Kenneth Starr had personally assisted Paula Jones' attorneys with their court challenge to presidential immunity from civil suits. So Kenneth Starr was now in the unheard-of position of "independently investigating" charges against a man he helped file a lawsuit against. But in Republican politics in the 1990's, all it took was a majority of one party devoid of any ethics or restraint to keep the inquisition going.

Starr had the FBI wire Linda Tripp to record her face-to-face conversations with Monica on several occasions. But, when even this extreme measure did not produce any incriminating evidence, Starr decided to set up a sting operation. On January 16, 1998, Starr had Linda Tripp meet her "friend," Monica Lewinsky, for lunch at the Ritz-Carlton hotel. Linda Tripp was again wired, but as soon as it was determined that the resultant conversation would not produce anything incriminating, the FBI moved in and arrested Monica Lewinsky. Ms. Tripp pretended to also be a victim of the sting, as she hugged Monica goodbye. But, as Monica was lead away in handcuffs, Linda Tripp went shopping. While Ms. Tripp spent the next few hours wandering the mall, Monica Lewinsky was subjected to 12 hours of interrogation in a room with up to nine FBI agents and OIC staff members.

Monica Lewinsky made repeated requests to call her attorney and her mother. But, her tormenters responded by mocking her, saying, "You're 24, you have to make a decision. You don't need to call your mommy." Refusing a person in custody their request for a lawyer is of course unconstitutional, but by now, such practices had become standard operating procedure for the Office of Independent Counsel.

Lewinsky's crime as near as anyone has been able to determine to this day was that she had an affair with the president of the United States. A president the American people had overwhelmingly re-elected to a second term, but whom conservative Republicans did not like. This was just another example of their politics by other means.

A meeting was held at midnight on the day Monica Lewinsky was arrested between members of Starr's team and Paula Jones attorneys.

The purpose of the meeting was to hatch a plot to entrap the president in his deposition for the Paula Jones lawsuit the next day, and then use it as a pretext for impeachment.

Keep in mind this elaborate sting operation conducted by the Office of Independent Counsel and the FBI was all for the benefit of a civil suit—not a criminal investigation, except for the fact that Kenneth Starr was calling it a criminal investigation. It was also aimed against a president who was supposed to be the leader of the very government these agencies were supposed to be a part of.

Forgetting the specific personalities involved for a moment, the fact that such extraordinary efforts and resources were being utilized against a sitting president would give the impression to most objective people that a political coup was indeed being perpetrated. Especially since this entire effort from beginning to end was totally engineered, financed and pushed exclusively by the political opponents of the president.

Paula Jones' attorneys in the Washington office of his attorney, Robert Bennett, questioned the president under oath the next day. The president was lawyerly evasive and parsed every word in his deposition, just as he has been accused of doing. And Paula Jones' attorneys may well have intentionally provided him with a vague definition of "sexual relations," knowing full well that he would seize the opportunity. Legally, the president's testimony may have been accurate, but in the court of public opinion, which is the audience Starr desperately needed to bring along, the hope was it would look exactly like what it was, a less-than-candid testimony. Testimony not designed to cover up any criminal wrongdoing, but rather a sexual tryst for which there was no legitimate reason to investigate to begin with.

As soon as Starr's investigation of the president's affair with Monica Lewinsky was well underway, the Paula Jones lawsuit was abruptly dismissed. The reason for dismissal was Ms. Jones' failure to prove that she suffered any damage due to the incident in question. The civil suit being dismissed would not of course end the sex investigation it spawned.

Meanwhile, Starr's sex investigation continued to spiral out of control, devoid of any restraint or decency. Kenneth Starr compelled a 24-year-old woman to divulge the most intimate details of her sex life. He terrorized her mother until she required sedation. He successfully convinced a conservative Supreme Court to compel secret service agents to break their long code of silence regarding a president's private life. When the president mentioned the possibility of invoking executive privilege regarding some material, instead of letting the Court rule on the matter as had always previously been the case, Starr immediately threatened to charge the president with contempt of court. And for the coupe de grace, Kenneth Starr would challenge a cornerstone of the American legal system in attempting to overturn the age-old precedent of client-lawyer confidentiality, in an attempt to interrogate the president's own White House counsel.

On September 9, 1998, Starr delivered to Congress an extraordinary, sexually graphic, 453-page document, suggesting 11 possible grounds for impeachment related to Clinton's attempts to cover up his sexual peccadillo.

Three days later in a hurried party line vote, the Republican-controlled Judiciary Committee opted to dump the entire contents of the Starr report onto the Internet. The report overflowed with graphic accounts of alleged sexual escapades in the Oval Office. Ironically, congressional conservatives would be responsible for releasing what was by far the most pornographic document ever published by the United States Government.

All of the heavy handed and unethical tactics employed by Kenneth Starr and congressional Republicans were appalling to most of America. As a result, in virtually every public opinion poll not commissioned by the Republican National Committee, greater than 60 percent of the American people consistently expressed their displeasure with the continued pursuit of the president. But, just as it had cost them the last two presidential elections, the Republican Party had once more been hijacked by its extreme, right-wing faction and the party could not bring itself to stop the runaway train of investigations of the president. As a result, Republicans lost 5 congressional seats instead of gaining 10 as expected in the mid-term election of 1998. Because of those loses, Newt Gingrich was through as Speaker of the House and would announce his resignation from the congressional seat he was just so easily re-elected to.

On December 12, 1998, the House Judiciary Committee approved four articles of impeachment along straight party line votes. Article I was for perjury in grand jury testimony, Article II for perjury in the Paula Jones civil deposition, Article III for obstruction of justice, and Article IV for perjury to Congress with regards to his answers to 81 written questions submitted to him by the House Judiciary Committee.

Starr based the obstruction-of-justice charge on his assertion of witness tampering. The witness tampering, in turn, was based on the premise that he lied to his secretary, Betty Currie, knowing that she would likely repeat what he told her if asked. The fact that Betty Currie was not on any list as a witness at the time of the alleged tampering made no difference. The obstruction charge was also based on Starr's conclusion that the president had agreed to get Monica Lewinsky a job in return for her keeping quiet about their affair. This despite the fact that Ms. Lewinsky testified repeatedly that no one ever offered her a job in return for her silence.

All of the perjury charges basically came down to the president not saying what Starr and congressional Republicans wanted to hear. In his grand jury testimony, the president admitted he had inappropriate, intimate contact with Monica Lewinsky of a physical nature. He also acknowledged it was wrong. But the president refused to give every humiliating detail. The one item that Starr and congressional Republicans have most publicized is the president's denial in his deposition of having "sexual relations" with Monica. This denial was based on the controversial definition of what constituted "sexual relations" provided by Jones' attorneys. A definition even the presiding judge stated was flawed.

To carry any legitimacy, any impeachment of an American president must be a bipartisan effort. It was with Watergate, it was anything but with what would come to be known as Zippergate. The Iran-Contra Affair, where the Reagan Administration traded arms for hostages and continued to wage a secret war against Nicaragua even after Congress voted to end it in 1982, was arguably an impeachable offense. Democrats were left fuming, but for the benefit of the nation, they went along with not pursuing impeachment when the administration agreed to stop the offensive action.

With regards to the Clinton impeachment, there was great concern throughout the country about a Republican coup to bring down the president. On February 13, 1998, a number of federal prosecutors, both Democrat and Republican expressed concern over the Starr's questionable tactics. One well-known attorney, William Ginsburg, stated that congressional Republicans had become "an anti-constitutional monster driven by a personal agenda to destroy the president."

Over 400 historians and 400 law professors signed and sent statements to Congress opposing the impeachment process due to the alleged charges not rising to the level of the high crimes clause of the constitution. They were ignored.

Then if things weren't weird enough, into the battle of smut jumped a professional—Larry Flynt, the owner and publisher of Hustler magazine. Flynt took a full page out in *The Washington Post* offering one million dollars for documented evidence of any illicit affair involving a member of Congress or other high government official. And information he got. House Speaker Newt Gingrich, in addition to leaving his first wife for another woman while she was dying of cancer, was now cheating on his present wife with a young, congressional clerk.

Speaker of the House—Designate Bob Livingston was discovered to have had an affair as well, as was chairman of the House Judiciary

Committee and chief Clinton prosecutor, Henry Hyde. When asked about the obvious hypocrisy, Hyde conveniently pronounced that, "the statute of limitations have long since passed on my youthful indiscretions." This despite the fact that his "youthful indiscretion" took place when he was 41 years of age, lasted for five years and only ended when the woman's husband confronted Hyde. Hyde's dalliance would result in the breakup of the woman's marriage. Many other Republicans were worrying over who would be "Flynted" next.

Shortly after 9:00 a.m. on December 17, 1998, Representative Ray Lahood of Illinois gaveled the House's impeachment hearing to order. Conspicuous by their absence were Speaker of the House Newt Gingrich and Speaker of the House-Designate Bob Livingston, both now tainted by adulterous affairs of their own.

LaHood then laid out the ground rules for the impeachment hearing, some of which were quite conveniently designed by the Republican leadership, such as being prohibited from drawing any comparisons between the president and any sitting member of Congress, such as Gingrich, Livingston or Hyde.

The proceeding began with Henry Hyde taking the podium and saying, "The matter before us is not about sex, adultery or even lying about sex, but lying under oath about it." He then cautioned that the impeachment was not what half of the Congress and most of America believed it to be, "the ravings of some vindictive political crusade, but an affirmation of a set of values that are tarnished and dim these days. The president is our flag bearer...the flag is falling," then he beseeched the Congress to, "catch the falling flag."

At the completion of Hyde's remarks, half of the House stood and applauded loudly—the Republican half, only serving to underscore the flaw of the whole process. It was exactly what Hyde had claimed it not to be.

The next two days saw a steady stream of House Representatives stating their opinions for history and the folks back home. Much of the harshest criticism of the president came from members of his own party, only to be followed by them stating their belief that as wrong as the president might have been, the penalty they were considering seemed grossly disproportionate to what was warranted by a stable government.

Congresswoman Rosa DeLauro of Conneticut called the entire process a "constitutional assassination." John Conyers called it "a Republican Coup d'etat."

The second day of the proceeding began with a bombshell that no one anticipated. Speaker of the House—Designate Bob Livingston first called on the president to do the noble thing and resign, and then committed political hari kari himself by announcing that he would not stand for the speaker-ship, but instead would follow his predecessor, Newt Gingrich, in resigning from the House of Representatives.

Minority Leader Dick Gephardt went to the podium some time later to speak of the turmoil, which seemed to be racing out of control. "We are at the brink of the abyss. The only way to stop this insanity is through the force of our own goodwill." Again, half of the House stood and applauded—the Democratic half, indicating there would be no change of heart, not that anyone expected there to be this late in the game.

After the debate, any Republican who had not decided on impeachment was treated to a private viewing of material gathered by the OIC. This included material of an unreported rape that the president supposedly committed 20 years ago, as well as other unsubstantiated material and innuendo, much of which had no relevance to the impeachment charges.

With all said and done, the House voted on the Articles of Impeachment in a rare Saturday session. Article I, Grand Jury Perjury, passed 228 to 206. Article II, Perjury in a Civil Deposition, was rejected 229 to 205. Article III, Obstruction of Justice, passed 221 to 212, and Article IV, Perjury to Congress, rejected 285 to 145.

At 1:25 p.m. on December 19, 1998, Bill Clinton became only the second American president impeached in history.

Even many moderate Republicans got caught up in the impeachment frenzy. But, feeling the heat from their constituents, 4 Republicans, including Sherwood Boehlert, Benjamin Gilman, Mike Castle, and Jim Greenwood, hedged their bets by voting for impeachment, then writing a letter to the Senate advising against conviction.

In response to his impeachment, President Clinton vowed he would continue working on what the people wanted done "until the last hour of the last day of my term."

The spotlight then shifted to the Senate where the trial of the president would take place. Senate historian Robert Byrd of West Virginia and many others were moribund at the prospect of vivid descriptions of sex acts being given in the Senate chamber. Majority Leader Trent Lott and others were appalled at the estimate of a trial lasting 4 months. So, Trent Lott and Minority Leader Tom Daschle began meeting to decide not how to conduct a fair trial, but rather how best to end it so as to limit any further damage and prevent sullying the Senate.

The Senate convened to begin the impeachment trial of President William Jefferson Clinton shortly after 2:00 p.m. on January 7, 1999. President Pro Tempore Strom Thurmond swore in the Chief Justice of the United States, William Renquist, for the trial. Then the Senate took the oath and signed a pledge to "do impartial justice." The pens used to sign the pledge, which were specially made for the occasion, underscored the flaw of the whole process. Instead of saying "United States Senator," they said "Untied States Senator." With no idea of exactly what to do next, the Senate then adjourned.

The following day the entire Senate met in the old senate chamber to attempt to forge a bipartisan deal for how the trial would be run. It was eventually decided that each side would be given 24 hours for opening arguments over three days. There would be two days where senators could submit questions in writing to be asked of either side by the chief justice. After that, a motion to dismiss or call witness would be made. Amazingly, the format passed 100 to zero.

On Thursday, January 14, 1999, Henry Hyde in his capacity as chief prosecutor read the two articles of impeachment passed by the House to the senate jury. After each article, he intoned, "William Jefferson Clinton has undermined the integrity of his office, has brought disrepute on the presidency, has betrayed his trust as president, and has acted in a manner subversive of the rule of law and justice, to the manifest injury of the people of the United States. Wherefore, William Jefferson Clinton, by such conduct, warrants impeachment and trial, and removal from office...."

As the trial began, bombs continued to rain down on Republicans, compliments of Larry Flynt. Signed affidavits were distributed to the press stating that Congressman and House Prosecutor Bob Barr had had an affair with his third wife while still married to his first wife. But even more explosive was an affidavit signed by his first wife that Barr— a staunch anti-abortion conservative—had paid for and even drove her to get an abortion back in 1983.

Henry Hyde made his opening statement on January 14. "We must never tolerate one law for the Ruler, and another for the Ruled. If we do, we break faith with our ancestors from Bunker Hill, Lexington and Concord to Flanders Field, Normandy, Iwo Jima, Panmunjon, Saigon, and Desert Storm."

"We are the heirs of the Ten Commandments and the Mosaic law...we are the heirs of Roman law...we are the heirs of the Magna Carta...Across the river in Arlington Cemetery, there are American heroes who died in defense of the rule of law. Can we give less than the full measure of our devotion to that great cause?"

Former Senator Dale Bumpers, of the president's home state of Arkansas, gave the opening statement for the defense. "We are here because of a five-year, relentless, unending investigation of the president. Fifty million dollars, hundreds of FBI agents fanning across the nation examining in detail the microscopic lives of people, maybe the most intense investigation not only of a president but of anybody, ever. But after all of those years and $50 million of Whitewater, Travelgate, Filegate, you name it—nothing, nothing—the president was found guilty of nothing, official or personal."

"When you hear somebody say, 'This is not about sex,' it's about sex. But there's a human element in this case that has not even been mentioned, and that is the president and Hillary and Chelsea are human beings. There's been nothing but sleepless nights, mental agony for this family for almost five years. Day after day, from accusations of having assassinated, or having had Vince Foster assassinated on down. It has been bizarre. We are none of us perfect. Sure, you say, he should have thought of all that beforehand. And indeed he should. Just as Adam and Eve should have…none of us are perfect. The people are saying, 'Please don't protect us from this man, 76 percent of us think he's doing a fine job; 65 to 70 percent of us don't want him removed from office.'"

Bumpers then concluded by challenging Henry Hyde's conclusion of what American soldiers had died for, telling the Senate that those Americans that made the supreme sacrifice did not do so, so they could overturn a democratic election over a personal indiscretion.

After a thirty-six day trial was capped off by four days of closed-door debate, the Senate voted 55 to 45 against the charge of perjury and 50 to 50 on the charge of obstruction of justice. With removal of the president from office requiring a two-thirds majority, Chief Justice William Renquist gaveled the trial adjourned at 12:39 p.m. on February 12, 1999, acquitting the president of all charges against him.

In 1974, congressional investigations into Watergate determined that President Nixon had used federal intelligence and law enforcement agencies to harass his political enemies and cover up acts of political espionage.

Conversely, in 1998, America witnessed a vengeful and out-of-control Congress perpetrate what amounted to a political coupe d' etat against a president of the opposition party. Because they had a simple majority of votes and the will to do so, they installed a rogue prosecutor. They then extensively and inappropriately used the combined investigative and law enforcement resources of the federal government in a thinly veiled attempt to overturn the result of democratic election they did not like. In the final analysis, Kenneth Starr and his congressional Republican sponsors ran roughshod over the Constitution and broke more laws in their pursuit of the president than they claimed to be investigating.

# Bibliography

Milestones—200 years of America Law by Jethro Liegerman (Oxford University Press, New York/ West publishing Company, St Paul)

Basic Cases in Constitutional Law, second edition by Duane Lockard and Walter F. Murphy (Congressional Quarterly Press, Princeton University)

The Boss, J. Edgar Hoover and the Great American Inquisition by Athan G. Theoharis and john Stuart Cox, Published by Bantam Books.

The Boss by Dayton David McKean.
Published by Houghton Mifflin Co.

Chronicle of America, Chronical Publication

The Federalist Era by John C. Miller. Published by Harper & Row.—Alien & Sedition Acts

Gideon's Trumpet by Anthony Lewis
Published by Random House

Miami and the Seige of Chicago by Norman Mailer
Published by Signet

A Thousand Days, John F. Kennedy in the White House
By Arthur M. Schlesinger
Published by Houghton Mifflin Co.

The Supreme Court Reporter
Hague, Mayor vs. Committee for Industrial Organization.
Hardwick vs. Bower.
Mapp vs. Ohio
Gideon vs. Wainwright
Gobitis vs. Minersville Board of Education
Hirabayashi vs. United States
Yasui vs. United States
Korematsu vs. United States

From Parlor to Prison
By Sherna Gluck
Published by Vintage Books

Susan B. Anthony
By Alma Lutz
Published by Beacon Press

Elizabeth Cady Stanton—A Radical for Women's Rights
By Lois W. Banner
Published by Little, Brown

The Congressional Record

The Debates and Proceedings in the Congress of the United States

The Bucks County Courier Times

Time Magazine

Newsweek

0-595-23912-9